**"Believe me, this stuff works in real life.** I am an attorney and CPA in Austin, Texas, and on a part-time basis I operate a statewide Christian grassroots organization. In effect, I oversaw the laboratory that experimented with these techniques and tested many of these ideas. We've learned a lot of things in the school of hard knocks. To do the things described in this book requires a lot of blood, sweat, and tears—in plain terms, hard work. But Charles Phillips has written a recipe for success, not an ivory-tower treatise."

—E. Adrian Van Zelfden
*President, Texas Grassroots Coalition*

"I watched how Charles Phillips used some of the techniques in this book to assist me in winning the Republican primary election for governor in Texas in the spring of 1990. Charlie helped me, and I think other candidates would be wise to make grassroots organizing an important part of their campaigns. This book is basically about how to recruit, train, and build people who believe in strong traditional values into an effective political force. I think that if more good, solid people in the communities will become involved in politics, we will turn our country back to greatness."

—Clayton W. Williams, Jr.
*1990 Republican Candidate for Governor of Texas*

# THE BLUE BOOK
## —— FOR ——
# GRASSROOTS POLITICS

## CHARLES R. PHILLIPS

A Division of Thomas Nelson Publishers
*Nashville*

Published in Nashville, Tennessee, by Oliver-Nelson Books, a division of Thomas Nelson, Inc., Publishers, and distributed in Canada by Lawson Falle, Ltd., Cambridge, Ontario.

Unless otherwise noted, the Bible version used in this publication is THE NEW KING JAMES VERSION. Copyright © 1979, 1980, 1982, Thomas Nelson, Inc., Publishers. Scripture quotations noted NASB are from the New American Standard Bible, © 1960, 1962, 1963, 1968, 1971, 1972, 1973, 1975, 1977 by The Lockman Foundation. Used by permission. Scripture quotations noted RSV are from the Revised Standard Version of the Bible, copyrighted 1946, 1952, © 1971, 1973. Verses marked TLB are taken from *The Living Bible*, copyright 1971 by Tyndale House Publishers, Wheaton, IL. Used by permission. Scripture quotations marked NIV are taken from the HOLY BIBLE: NEW INTERNATIONAL VERSION. Copyright © 1973, 1978, 1984 by the International Bible Society. Used by permission of Zondervan Bible Publishers. Scripture quotations noted JERUSALEM BIBLE are from THE JERUSALEM BIBLE, copyright © 1966 by Darton, Longman & Todd Ltd. and Doubleday & Company, Inc. Used by permission.

Printed in the United States of America.

ISBN 0-8407-9572-6

1 2 3 4 5 6 — 95 94 93 92 91 90

*To*
*those people who God calls to meet the needs*
*of His servants, those who are out of the mold*
*of "the widow of Zaraphat":*
Mr. Frank Hester,
*who was faithful to see God's work done*
*went to be with the Lord after the 1988 presidential primary.*
*His lovely wife,* Sarah, *is continuing the work*
*in such a valiant way.*
*The support, prayers, and backing of*
Josh *and* Lorraine Ewing
*lifted my arms in times of weakness.*

*These two couples and others like them*
*are like the pillars in a foundation, unseen,*
*that are the very strength and stability*
*of that which is visible.*

# Contents

About the Author    ix
Acknowledgments    xi
Preface    13

1. To Serve in the King's Court    21
2. Nonprofit Organizations for Political Action    35
3. Political Action Committees    55
4. Mobilizing the Christian PAC    75
5. The Pastors' Coalition    107
6. The Campaign Strategy    131
7. Implementing the Strategy    159
8. Election Day    177

    Appendixes:
A  A Glossary of Political Offices    185
B  An Overview of Party Convention Procedures    189
C  Technology at the Grassroots    203
D  A Biblical Study: Leadership, Morality, and
    Freedom    211

# About the Author

Charles R. Phillips has been in and around the political scene since 1967. He began his active involvement when he became political committee chairperson of the two-thousand-member Junior Chamber of Commerce in Houston, Texas. In 1968 Phillips became associate director of the Texas Attorney General's Youth Conference Against Crime. He traveled throughout Texas speaking to high school and college students as part of an antidrug-abuse project. In addition, he created teen courts and other programs addressing issues pertinent to youth. Under Phillips' supervision, 138 local youth council chapters were established and 1,500 youth delegates were sent to a three-day summer conference at the state capital. The program's structure and success became a model for other states undertaking similar projects.

In 1970 Preston Smith, the governor of Texas, asked Charles Phillips to become executive director of the Governor's Conference of College Leaders. The purpose of the program was to help defuse tension on college campuses and to establish direct communication between campus student leaders and the governor's office.

For the following three years Charles Phillips worked on political campaigns and programs. In 1975, however, he chose to enter the private sector in agriculture, and his political involvement became a hobby for the next eleven years.

# About the Author

In 1986 Phillips reentered the political arena. He managed the last twelve weeks of David Davidson's campaign for lieutenant governor, organizing over one hundred Texas counties and raising $180,000.

The Coalition of Politically Active Christians (COPAC) was born from that campaign, mobilizing four thousand volunteers in more than two hundred Texas counties. Members of COPAC created a Judeo-Christian voter identification file comprising over one hundred fifty thousand families at the county and precinct levels. Phillips has used this file to help elect candidates ranging from county commissioner, small city mayor, and community action board member to state representative justice on the Texas Supreme Court, and governor. Since its inception, COPAC has recruited and trained over fifteen hundred people to run for party offices throughout Texas and the United States. He has managed or been consulted on 14 races for school board, mayor, county commissioner, lieutenant governor, governor, Texas Supreme Court, U.S. Senate, U.S. House of Representatives, and state representative.

Charles Phillips' desire has been to take an active part in pulling down the strongholds of liberalism that have influenced America since the early seventies. His intention is not to make Americans Democrats or Republicans, nor is it to promote one doctrinal view over another or to create a theocracy. His intention is to call America to return to a foundation of righteousness.

Phillips' vision is to regain a balance of power with liberals by educating and uniting Judeo-Christian traditional-values voters who believe in and adhere to the Constitution of the United States and who believe the United States to be a republic. His goal is to utilize his God-given talents and energy to help unite Christian political activists and turn them into a movement.

Dwight L. Moody had a favorite saying, "The world has not yet seen what one man can do, who is fully committed to God." Think what the world would see if a corporate body of voters were fully committed to God!

☆ x ☆

# Acknowledgments

**O**ver the past decade there have been those warriors, valiant men and women who heard the trumpet sound and answered the call to defend our freedoms and godly inheritance.

Their work has been a personal inspiration. We all owe a debt of gratitude to Dr. James Dobson, Focus on the Family; Dr. Tim LaHaye, American Coalition for Traditional Values; Dr. Pat Robertson; Dr. D. James Kennedy; Mrs. Beverly LaHaye, Concerned Women of America; Mrs. Phyllis Shafley, Eagle Forum; Dr. David Balsinger, Biblical News Service; Col. Donor, Christian Voice Foundation; Dr. Bob Grant, Christian Voice; Dr. Jerry Falwell, Moral Majority; Paul Wyrich, Free Congress Foundation; Gary Bauer, Family Research Council; and Mark Nuttle, R.N.C.C. I know there are a hundred more that have defended our heritage.

Those who personally aided me in making this book possible include Mike Ruston; Adrian Van Zelfden, Texas Grassroots Coalition; Dennis Spillman, and Richie Martin.

I thank Norman Anderson, Rita Davis, and Rosie Martinez who put in so many hours working on this manual and Mr. Harold Turner for his tireless efforts.

To those who supported my family and me spiritually and financially—Rev. Dewey "Bud" Gardner, Dr. and Mrs. Michael Dwyer, Mr. Robert Johnson, and Mrs. Martha Armstrong—I am

# Acknowledgments

so grateful. God sent these people who were so faithful while standing with us in the campaigns.

To my beloved wife and children—your sacrifice and encouragement made this book possible.

For we wrestle not against flesh and blood, but against principalities, against powers, against the rulers of the darkness of this world, against spiritual wickedness in high places (Eph. 6:12 KJV).

# Preface

In America we are presently seeing the results of what happens when Christians ignore their civic responsibilities. As a nation we have forgotten that our political foundations were laid by God. In their book *The Light and the Glory,* Peter Marshall and David Manuel did excellent work documenting that America did not just happen but was God-ordained.[1] The true hope of America for the twenty-first century lies in the return of God's people to their corporate covenant with God. To this end we must elect officials who acknowledge the sovereign power and authority of God over man. As David admonished: "Now therefore, be wise, O kings; be instructed, you judges of the earth. Serve the LORD with fear, and rejoice with trembling. Kiss the Son, lest He be angry, and you perish in the way, when His wrath is kindled but a little. Blessed are all those who put their trust in Him" (Ps. 2:10–12).

Unknown to many Americans, a religion of humanism prevails within our political system. A battle is raging between humanistic forces and the Christian religious community. Humanism prevails because we have allowed it to prevail. For example, within our educational system Horace Mann, secretary of the Massachusetts Board of Education, introduced humanism

---

1. Peter Marshall and David Manuel, *The Light and the Glory* (Old Tappan, N.J.: Fleming Revell, 1977).

to nineteenth-century American education. Mann supported forced taxation for state schools, which undermined parental control and was detrimental to private schools. He subtly tore away at the biblical doctrine of salvation as the basis of character development and replaced it with the optimistic, humanistic view of the perfectibility of man through education. He also standardized teachers' training, textbooks, and accreditation, thus institutionalizing a humanist ideology.

If freedom of religion is to be retained in the United States and passed on as an inheritance to our children, then we must actively organize to elect godly men and women to public office. We must not forsake our part of God's covenant and commandment to us as a nation. The United States cannot simply rely on being just a moral nation.

The Reverend S. W. Foljambe said on January 5, 1876: "The more thoroughly a nation deals with its history, the more decidedly will it recognize and own an overruling providence therein, and the more religious a nation will it become; while the more superficially it deals with its history seeing only secondary causes and agencies, the more irreligious will it be."

Did the founding fathers truly intend to separate religion from state? The founding fathers did not believe in nor did they practice "separation of church and state"— at least not in the way it is presented by the American Civil Liberties Union (ACLU) and humanists today. The founding fathers were mindful of official state churches in Europe where people were not free to worship as they desired. Thus, the first amendment of the Constitution states: "Congress shall make no law respecting an establishment of religion, or prohibiting the free exercise thereof." People were to be able to worship according to their beliefs as long as they did not infringe on other people's constitutional rights. The government was not created to protect us from protestant or evangelical values, as is propagandized today by liberal groups.

From 1980 to the present, the conservative religious community's involvement in politics as a special interest group has gone through a revolutionary process. To understand that process, we must first review some American political history.

Prior to World War I, the Christian community was involved in the American political arena. However, after the evangelical churches supported Herbert Hoover for president and the Great Depression followed, the church developed a hands-off policy toward American politics and taught that God ordained the rulers over us (see Rom. 13). Therefore, the Christian community was to follow whatever legislation the government had set forth, even if it was contrary to biblical principles.

After World War II, American political ideology moved farther from the Bible as the inspiration for legislative government. Legislators started accepting the beliefs of humanists as given in the *Humanist Manifesto*, which purported that every situation or problem could be solved by man. Our country moved toward man-centeredness rather than God-centeredness. The prevalent philosophy during the sixties was rebellion and "if it feels good do it."

The liberal church, promoting causes such as human rights, became involved in American politics while the conservative church remained aloof. The conservative church forfeited prayer in school, and the traditional values that had dominated our society began to dissipate in the face of secular humanist philosophy. While this change was taking place in the sixties and the "God Is Dead" movement was on the forefront, a new awakening took place—the Jesus movement. The charismatic (or renewal) movement followed on its heels.

The seventies brought an end to mainline denominations influencing political affairs. Secular humanists took over the Democratic party and began to pass liberal laws. The Supreme Court moved to the left and adopted a secular humanist agenda, which legalized abortion, championed the rights of the criminal at the expense of the victim, and helped establish the women's liberation movement and homosexual rights. Secular humanists, with the help of the media and the academic community, defined *eu-thanasia* as "death with dignity," *homosexuality* as "an alternative lifestyle," and life in a mother's womb as "a mass of meaningless tissue."

The lesbians and homosexuals have a well-planned, well-financed political and social agenda. U.S. Congressman William Dannemeyer sums up the battle in his book, *Shadow in the Land:* "The political activities of the homosexual community have become so effective that we are at a point in our era where, unless we're willing to affirm the heterosexual ethic of our society, the homosexual movement will win—they will win by default."

President Jimmy Carter was the first major political candidate in decades to consider the evangelical community as a special-interest group that could be important in electing a candidate through the grassroots process. President Carter's claim to be "born again" was a rallying point for the silent majority who had been looking for a champion to offset liberal influences in politics. Many conservatives became extremely disappointed when they found those words were just rhetoric of a person with a socialistic or humanistic mind-set who believed compromise was the solution to the world's problems and who put conviction on the altar as a sacrifice.

In 1980 Ronald Reagan, the actor-statesman turned politician, was ready to position himself as the new champion of the "religious right." Defined as such by the news media, this newly emerged special interest group was most visible as the Moral Majority led by the Reverend Jerry Falwell. Other leaders on the scene were Howard Phillips of the Religious Round Table; Dr. Tim LaHaye of the American Coalition for Traditional Values; Phyllis Shafley, Eagle Forum; Dr. Pat Robertson of the Christian Broadcasting Network; Dr. Robert Grant of the Christian Voice; and Paul Wyrich of the Heritage Foundation.

Through skilled oratory and the activities of those new grassroots special-interest groups, Ronald Reagan won the presidency easily. In 1984 President Reagan again counted on those groups to be active at the grassroots level and win over the independent vote. He won handily and carried on his coattails many other candidates.

In 1986 the old guard believed that this new group would vote Republican even without Republican candidates addressing issues concerning Judeo-Christian traditional values. The Republican old guard should have learned from 1982 when many statewide races were run with the same strategy and many Republican candidates went down in defeat. The Congressional candidates of 1986 met a similar fate.

These powerful grassroots groups then began to develop local identity. The religious right had formed local political organizations but maintained a 501(c)(3) mentality; that is, they maintained their status as tax deductible organizations. On the national level Beverly LaHaye's Concerned Women for America organization, Phyllis Shafley's Eagle Forum, and Pat Robertson's Freedom Council became dominant leaders, but both organizations were 501(c)(3) and 501(c)(4). The real power was Paul Wyrich's Council on National Policy. Their tax deductible status prevented them from involvement in grassroots politics. They were basically in the business of educating the electorate. Such organizations had not yet realized that forming political action committees (PACs) was necessary to do political work. The grassroots of the Judeo-Christian movement relied on newsletters and voter report cards as their main political tools.

Then in 1986 the unexpected happened. Viable candidates began to emerge from the religious right. Joe Lutz ran in the Oregon Republican primary against Senator Packwood; David Davidson of Texas ran for lieutenant governor against Democrat Lieutenant Governor Bill Hobby. At least twenty-five other traditional-values candidates were on the ballot around the nation. Each of these challengers was similar in that none was selected by a Republican candidate recruitment committee to run. Each was under-financed and had to run a totally grassroots campaign, and each faced a favored liberal incumbent. Many of these challengers did remarkably well. Local groups began to form PACs.

Because national Christian organizations were 501(c)(3)1, they could not use their mailing lists, finances, and leadership to campaign actively against candidates that supported abortion, gay rights, and other issues. They had not fully learned that to make a lasting effect on politicians and legislation, defeating the liberal leadership in the national and state legislatures was required.

The conservative Christian religious right was still more of a mob than an organized political movement. That was never more evidenced than by the Robertson campaign for the presidency. The religious right was manipulated by established Republicans and the press. But because of Pat Robertson's campaign for president, even more charismatics and evangelicals became involved in the political process than ever before. An interesting result of Robertson's campaign was the influence on local party politics. Thousands of people supporting Judeo-Christian traditional values won their precinct chairmanship, the local county chair, and the state Republican executive committee position. They even took control of entire state party organizations from moderate and liberal Republicans.

In 1988 George Bush took the religious right away from Jack Kemp and Pat Robertson. As president, George Bush united the religious or Christian traditional-values coalition into the largest single coalition behind any modern-day candidate. Bush utilized prime time TV and Reagan speech writers to strengthen his hold on the conservative vote by delivering a message that pulled together many special-interest groups.

From its formation during the 1986 elections, the Coalition of Politically Active Christians developed most of the strategies and methods described in this book. We have computerized the names of thousands of Christian voters, categorizing them by precinct, state representative districts, and congressional districts. COPAC has recruited and trained people to run for party positions and local offices, from mayor to congressional representative. We established a pastors' coalition on traditional values and learned what pastors wanted to know about the political process and the current issues confronting us. COPAC has also spent time and finances researching voting trends of the Christian community as well as the proper role and function of Christian political action committees.

We have learned to clarify the nature of our involvement, which we found was not based upon Republican or secular issues, but rather upon biblical teachings concerning abortion, pornography, parental rights, humanism, freedom of religion, and homosexuality. Judeo-Christian traditional values became the plumb line of our involvement.

Across the nation, the religious right as a special-interest group has started to work together and mature. Organizations such as CPPC, led by Dennis Peacock, head of CPPC and Focus on the Family, led by Dr. James Dobson and Dr. D. James Kennedy, are moving to the forefront. Dr. Pat Robertson has formed the Christian Coalition out of this 1988 presidential bid. The newly emerged grassroots movement is preparing for the twenty-first century with new leadership and a new vision.

In 1980, 3 to 5 percent of the Texas Republican state convention could be identified as the religious right. By 1984, the number grew to between 8 and 10 percent; in 1986, the figure was 17 percent, and in 1988, the number of delegates identifying themselves with the religious right reached 44 percent. At the 1988 Texas Republican convention a coalition was formed between the Robertson delegates, COPAC, and Texas Grassroots, all of which are statewide Christian organizations. The purpose was to have a coordinated effort to elect our candidates to party positions and to support a conservative party platform. The effort was successful, which showed that cooperation was not compromise but rather the best method of operation. A similar effort by Mike Ruston led the Christian conservatives in Minnesota to a take-over of the state party. In 1984, when Mondale carried Minnesota, the religious right helped elect a majority of conservatives to the House of Representatives.

We saw the beginning of a national movement in 1988; we were no longer a mob, and we were coming into maturity. States that had strong, aggressive, organized Christian grassroots political action committees were for the first time electing state and local candidates.

The agenda of American politics is being set by the lesbian and gay PAC network, which is well-funded from industry, Hollywood, and individuals. Nationally those PACs are putting together between $20 million and $30 million dollars, as well as a very solid grassroots organization. You will find this network working from Washington down to your local city council. Over the last forty years they have taken control of key positions in the bureaucracy, in media, in finance, and as the support groups to politicians. You don't fight abortion; you can't destroy pornography. They are the results of an agenda to destroy the very moral fiber of America. If you destroy America's youth, you destroy America. America's always one generation away from atheism.

What, then, can networking do? It can turn an ineffective mob into an effective movement. I hope each section of this manual will help you, your church, or your interest group to form an effective political action committee.

We must remember that this nation was formed by thirteen small colonies banding together in unity with the goal of freedom and liberty. At the Constitutional Convention of 1787, Benjamin Franklin stood to say:

> The longer I live, the more convincing proofs I see of this truth, that God governs in the affairs of men. And if a sparrow cannot fall to the ground without His notice, is it probable that an empire can rise without His aid? We have been assured in the sacred writings that "except the Lord build the house, they labor in vain." I firmly believe this; and I also believe that, without His concurring aid, we shall succeed in this political building no better than the builders of Babel.

# To Serve in the King's Court

Can a righteous person serve in politics without losing his or her religious convictions? Herb Ellingwood, formerly with the White House staff during the Reagan era, stated in a meeting with traditional-values Christian leaders that given a person's position in Washington, D.C., one could indulge in all the perversion he desired.

What, then, are the principles one must adhere to in order to serve God with integrity in a system that denies God's sovereignty? One must first examine the person who is labeled a Christian candidate. The wisdom and integrity to serve in a political party or public office and make decisions based on biblical principles cannot be performed without prior knowledge and practice of those principles. In selecting leaders for any office, one must decide whether he or she is "blameless" in conduct (1 Tim. 5:7), "temperate, sober-minded, of good behavior, hospitable" (1 Tim. 3:2), "of a sound mind" (2 Tim. 1:7).

To be the minister described in Romans 13, one must have God's wisdom and understanding (the mind of Christ). This is consistent with the thinking of our forebears. For instance, prior to the nineteenth century a lawyer had to have a degree in theology before he could enter law school.

## Daniel's Example

The prophet Daniel did not compromise God's principles and applied them with steadfastness: "But Daniel purposed in his heart that he would not defile himself with the portion of the king's meat" (Dan. 1:8). Daniel was able to hear God in his heart, recognize God's voice, and stand alone in his loyalty to the word of God.

There are times when Christians—voters and candidates—must make decisions and stand firm, just as Daniel did.

God's gift of wisdom and understanding cannot be bought with silver and gold. One must discern where a candidate's wisdom is centered. Is it a secular understanding or a spiritual understanding? Has the person set aside human reasoning and striven to obtain God's wisdom? One must ask oneself before entering politics, "Is my nature God-centered or self-centered?" In Genesis we have the first account of reasoning that was self-centered and not God-centered. Human beings have always struggled against God's purposes and ways.

## The Role of Prayer

To follow the leadership or servant model set forth in the Bible by David, Daniel, Jesus, Paul, and John, one must spend time in prayer. Benjamin Franklin, a deist, recognized the need for prayer. During the Constitutional Convention, there was an impasse, and Franklin called for a moment of prayer.

Prior to the nineteenth century, colonial courts and government officials called many times for prayer and fasting when a major disaster or problem arose.

Modern Americans must realize, and stay loyal to, who truly has the power; we must know that God ordains and establishes the nations. David Barton's 1988 book *To Pray or Not to Pray* follows prayer and the role it has played in American history.

☆ **22** ☆

## Foundation Building in the Political System

The first colonial grant made to Sir Walter Raleigh in 1584 and the grant authorizing him to enact statutes for the government of a proposed colony provided that "they be not against the true Christian faith."[1]

A person cannot remain faithful or steadfast to his faith without an understanding and knowledge of a government ordained by God.

It seems that over the past decade the Judeo-Christian political effort has concentrated on high profile positions such as senator or congressman. While doing this, a solid grassroots political base has not been built. If we are truly to become effective in changing the government, we must learn from the Democrats the process of winning lesser offices to form a solid political foundation. We also have given our votes, money, and time to candidates without demanding proper recognition. Therefore, the candidates elected by us have not been made accountable for their promises. The foundation for a strong political movement is to build from the bottom up with candidates of integrity and principle who remain loyal to the people who help put them in office.

## The Political Party System

Political activity in America is concentrated in two parties: one consisting of Republicans and the other of Democrats. There have been third parties participating in America politics; however, they have never been a serious challenge to the major parties' candidates. Established voting patterns and demographics usually prohibit third parties from winning elections in America. Third-party politics in America is not truly in the interest of the Christian. If Christians would start a third party, demo-

---

1. David Barton, *To Pray or Not to Pray* (Fort Worth, 1988).

graphic projections indicate that the voter bloc would never be large enough to win major elections. Trying to establish a third party would dilute the conservative vote and in effect give most elected offices to liberals.

The necessity of winning elections makes imperative Christian participation in one of the two major parties. The Democratic party, however, is not open to conservative participation. At this time the Democrats use their credentials committees to exclude conservative participants. The Democratic platform reflects the ultraliberal influence of the party leadership. The extreme attitudes of Democrats toward social and moral issues have remained fixed even though national attitudes have changed. That inflexible position will become indefensible in the near future. The Democrats also have serious factional divisions within the party that are irreconcilable. The ultraliberal leadership will never concede their position. In the early nineties Democratic candidates will have only nominal success. However, that will begin to change as the party becomes more receptive to Judeo-Christian values.

The Republican party is not without problems. However, it is the logical choice for Christian participation in this decade. Because the Republican party has only within the last twenty years become viable in the politics of most states, there are vacant positions in party organizations across the nation. The platform reflects a morally conservative view influenced by recent Christian participation. If we concentrate our efforts in the Republican party, our effectiveness will be increased. If we choose the Democratic party, our efforts would be expended in factional party politics and little could be done to elect moral, conservative candidates. We still must fight party battles. However, the conservative influence in the Republican party can be cultivated to assist us in our objectives. That can be done by trading support for their candidates. This conservative/Christian coalition can and will dominate Republican party politics for years to come.

Presently, evangelical Christian voters are not an organized majority. The object of involving Christians in politics is to win elections with our candidates, and by winning elections we will change the humanist perspective of our present government. We must consolidate our numbers with conservative Republicans; then we must maintain that change by vigilant continuous participation. We must ensure that the government our children inherit is not hostile to an individual's liberty or to religious freedom.

When I talk of Judeo-Christian Republican involvement, I speak of this as one speaks of Goldwater Republicans and Reagan Republicans. *Evangelical Christian Republicans,* as defined by the media, would be the "vocal, activist, religious right." Of those citizens who believe abortion should be illegal, a survey conducted by American Christian Research and Education foundation in 1989 shows that 12 percent of this voting bloc were against any form of abortion except to save the life of the mother. Eight percent were against any form of abortion except for rape and to save the life of the mother. Twenty percent would allow abortion except for sex selection birth control, with parental and spousal consent. The press seems to relate to the 12 percent when it uses the term *religious right.*

Every moment we tarry, our children and our children's children are placed in jeopardy. Is their future to be given over to a value system of atheists and even taken from them by profiteering abortionists? Therefore, for effective political action to take place, Christians should participate in the Republican party. I do not, however, condemn those who participate in the Democratic party. God does not live anywhere without a witness. In His time the Democratic party will be changed.

Thus, logic dictates Christians with traditional values to go where the greatest advantage for influence exists; and today that is the Republican party. The 1988 national and state platforms of the Republican party reflect good, morally conservative positions. For example, they support pro-life, pro-family, and pro-American positions. Therefore, partisan involvement as individuals in the Republican party should be encouraged.

## Organizational Structure of the Republican Party

Let's begin with the basic political unit in Republican politics—the primary voter (see chart below). The primaries are open to all eligible voters. However, in a single election year you may vote in only one party's primary. Some states require registration as either a Republican or Democrat. Those voting in the Republican primary or participating in a caucus are Republican party members for that particular year. Republican primary voters make three important decisions: They choose the party's nominees for the general election, elect precinct chairpersons, and elect the Republican county chair.

### TYPICAL POLITICAL PARTY IN THE STATE

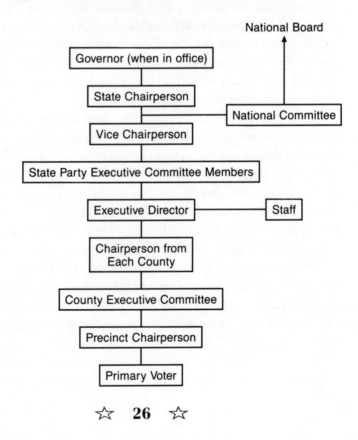

The precinct chairperson is responsible for informing and organizing the Republican primary voters in his or her precinct. Each precinct has approximately three to six thousand Republican voters. Usually the precinct chairperson will serve as election judge during primaries and general elections. The precinct chair also sits on the county executive committee.

The county executive committee usually meets quarterly and is composed of all the precinct chairpersons in the county and is administered by the party county chairperson. The executive committee is the most influential body in local party politics. The executive committee confirms or rejects actions of the county chairpersons and elects the temporary senatorial district chairperson by the senatorial district convention.

The county chairperson also raises monies for local party administration and activities. He or she usually influences candidate recruitment for county offices. The county chairperson should work in concert with the state party executive committee.

The state party executive committee (hereafter referred to as SREC, using the Republican as an example) is a state executive committee that runs the party between conventions. At the state convention, delegates caucus (or meet in groups) by state senatorial districts. The caucus will elect two SREC members—one man and one woman. The campaigns for SREC are run prior to the convention and candidacy should be determined in advance of the state convention. The SREC functions like the board of directors of a corporation and is chaired by the state party chairperson.

The state party chairperson is elected at the state convention. The senatorial caucus nominates a man and woman for each office—chair and vicechair. In most states, if the chair is a man, the vicechair must be a woman. The state chairperson is answerable to the SREC, and in most states the chairperson is usually receptive to counsel from the governor or the ranking elected party's U.S. Senator.

There are several governing conventions that shape the political party (see chart on page 26). These gatherings are the decision-making elements of local, state, and national politics. The delegates to these conventions decide what the party platform will be. They also decide who the candidate will be in presidential election years. The convention process begins at precinct level.

The precinct caucus is held at a designated time (usually 7:00 P.M.) after the party primary. The precinct caucus is held in the polling place, and most state party headquarters can tell you where and when it meets. To attend the Democratic or Republican precinct caucus you must have voted in that political party's primary election. In some states you must register as a Democrat or a Republican. The first order of business at the caucus is to select a temporary chairperson to conduct the election of the permanent caucus chairperson. (Note: this is not the precinct chairperson who is elected by the primary vote. The sole function of the caucus chairperson is to conduct this meeting and turn in the minutes.) After electing the chairperson, a secretary and a sergeant-at-arms are also elected. Any resolutions to amend the party platform are submitted for ratification at the precinct caucus by a majority of those present. After ratifying the resolutions, the delegates for the district convention are elected. Understand again, a majority of the delegates at the district or county convention are needed to pass resolutions and elect your delegates to the state convention. If you believe in a resolution, see to it that people who share your convictions are the majority of the people present to vote.

The delegates elected to the district or county convention decide which resolutions and which delegates go to the state convention. The state delegates will elect the state chair, vicechair, and SREC members. They draft and endorse a state party platform as well as elect delegates to the national convention. The national convention delegates nominate a presidential candidate and a vice-presidential candidate and adopt a national platform.

A very important action at a convention is the selection of delegates to the next convention. In 1984 presidential candidate

Gary Hart received the most votes in Democratic primaries, but lost the nomination to Mondale because his supporters did not appreciate the importance of sending delegates to the national convention. Thus, Hart lost the nomination at the precinct caucus level.

For Christians to win Republican party nominations, work must be done at the precinct caucus level.

Briefly, that is the party organizational structure and convention process. Although this process is similar in most states, I urge you to get your state's rules from the state party headquarters.

Apart from state differences, there are two keys to success in political party politics. First, and most important, know the rules by which the process is governed and learn *Robert's Rules of Order*. Second, know the players, their positions, and the scope of their influence.

## Knowing the Rules

The key to any form of competition is knowing the rules of engagement. Most folks enter politics without knowing the rules and become discouraged because they are exploited by the "old guard" who may not know the rules either but have the influence to override the rules. An individual who knows the rules can see that the rules are adhered to. The rules by which the Republican or Democratic party is administered come from three sources: the State Election Code, the rules of the state political party of [State], and *Robert's Rules of Order, Revised*.

To participate you only need to show up, but to be effective you must have a working knowledge of the rules. The Election Code can be obtained from your state election headquarters and usually from the Secretary of State in the state capital. The Republican or Democratic party rules can be obtained from your local county party headquarters or state party headquarters. *Robert's Rules of Order* may be obtained from a local bookstore.

A working knowledge of these rules is necessary for success. Motions have often failed in committee meetings for lack of a second motion, only because committee members did not know enough to realize that without a second the motion dies. Many times positions of influence go to men and women simply because they are proficient in parliamentary procedure. Instructions, therefore, should be given to all participants in the proper exercise of party procedures.

## Knowing the Players

The second key to effective political participation is to know who the players are and which side they play for. Perhaps the most difficult aspect of political activism is to discern friends from foes. Most of the old guard participants have run the party for a long time, and that's how they like it. They decide all questions of policy and disbursement of resources, and this group is typically, though not always, the liberal to moderate element of the party. Other people may be involved in party affairs for business reasons. Don't shy away from participation because of these elements. The reason we have to become involved is because these folks have been running things while we have warmed the church pews.

The best advice is to participate quietly and observe the players in motion. Try to find Christian activists who have been involved for a while and get briefed on who is who. If you are on your own, evaluate what motivates each individual. That, faster than anything else, will give you an indication of how people will act and react to the thing you would like to see the party do.

No man is an island. The people you are working with are your neighbors and fellow countrymen. You must live with them and evangelize them. This is, however, not a mandate for a theocracy. God is Sovereign in His own right. Nothing we can do or will do can add anything to that absolute sovereignty. If Christians come to politics with the attitude that their denomination is to dictate to the world God's divine will, we will all be wasting

God's resources. Therefore, let us work on common ground for common objectives.

## Participating for Change

We must participate for change and even revolutionary change. Remember, however, we did not become a humanist nation overnight, so change will not occur overnight. Do not condemn those who are involved in other areas of God's work for not giving their time to politics. God has not quickened each of us to the same responsibilities. However, voting for a Christian brother or sister who will take stands that promote traditional values is a Christian's responsibility to our Lord Jesus Christ. If we don't keep the "foxes out of the vineyard," who will?

We are not the majority, yet we can change the government through politics because those who do participate make the decisions. We must use the resources we have to gain the greatest influence, and party politics is the ideal mechanism to establish influence. This can be accomplished by recognizing the guiding principles Christians have in common. Regardless of background, you will find very few Christians who will argue against the basic tenets of God's revealed will. Let's acknowledge those common principles and allow them to shape our politics and government. The future of this nation will be changed by Christian involvement. The alternative may be to wake up one morning to find that freedom of religion no longer exists and the new state religion, secular humanism, is the only legal religion in America.

When areas of common concern are identified, Christians in politics must bring together groups and individuals within the party that share these concerns and form a coalition. If Christians cooperate with the moral and social conservatives of the party, there will be fewer losses on election day.

With such a coalition in control of the party, Christian candidates then have the necessary support guaranteed to put them on a competitive basis. Christians need the party for credibility and the party needs us for viability. The religious denomination of the chairperson is not as important as where he or she stands on the issue of abortion. A rule to follow is: Never compromise the Scripture, never break the Ten Commandments, and accept what the Lord gives. Remember, He did not give Israel the land on the day His promise was made to Abraham. His timing is perfect. Take the land when it is ready for possession.

## Organizing for Change

To return America to moral and spiritual sanity, both political parties must be influenced to endorse common Christian values. Our prayer for the future of our nation should be that the positions for which we are now fighting will one day be acknowledged by all Americans. That can be accomplished by Christians participating in Republican partisan politics as well as by supporting Democratic candidates with voting records that adhere to basic moral values. Candidates within the Republican party that do not follow the party platform should be *opposed* with votes. Collectively, you should have an organization that is bipartisan—a political action committee (PAC). Your PAC should endorse only Judeo-Christian traditional-values candidates. When the voters elect Republicans because they represent biblical values, the Democrats will either take on Judeo-Christian traditional values or they will cease to have a viable party. Change in extreme leftist positions will open the Democratic party to Christian participation. This should not, however, be the Christian's cue to exit politics. Freedom is maintained only by eternal vigilance in prayer and action. Therefore, we should participate indefinitely, because that is how values are perpetuated. Always remember that those who participate make the decisions and choices that affect us all. If we falter for only a brief period, our descendants may have to do what we are doing now. Worse, they may not have the opportunity or means to do it. Certainly, if we fail, tyranny will be their inheritance. Until King Jesus comes back, pray that we are not to be the ones who will report to Him that our inheritance has been squandered for lack of concern.

# Nonprofit Organizations for Political Action

Nonprofit organizations can be beneficial to the community and to a political agenda by serving, educating, and motivating conservative Christian voters. The new Christian right has chosen to use the Republican party as its main vehicle for political involvement, and there are many ways that a new Christian right nonprofit organization can establish a relationship with inactive members of the Republican party. The Republican party has a problem with many minority voters who hold traditional values because the Republican party has a reputation for ignoring the needs of certain voting blocs.

Why do the Hispanic, black, elderly, and rural voters persist in voting Democratic when the leaders of that party support liberal values that run contrary to the family values that those groups hold dear? Could this be a judgment on the church and parachurch groups for their lack of concern and action in regard to pressing social issues?

Conservative Christian nonprofit organizations can be politically effective by working to solve the social problems of this nation's citizens. At the same time we must be careful not to become involved in a socialist agenda or promote liberation theology. Instead we should have the heart of God toward all people facing injustice.

How more direct a command to the church from God than this passage from Isaiah explaining His heart's desire toward oppressed people?

> Is this not the fast that I have chosen:
> To loose the bonds of wickedness,
> To undo the heavy burdens,
> To let the oppressed go free,
> And that you break every yoke?
> Is it not to share your bread with the hungry,
> And that you bring to your house the poor
>   who are cast out;
> When you see the naked, that you cover
>   him? (Isa. 58:6–7).

We should realize that we can build godly relationships with neglected people by serving them, just as the Lord Jesus did. Let us be mindful of His example: "And Jesus, when He came out, saw a great multitude and was moved with compassion for them, because they were like sheep not having a shepherd. So He began to teach them many things" (Mark 6:34).

The Christian nonprofit organization is an effective vehicle for educating people about the political system and candidates' positions regarding pro-family issues.

As an Old Testament prophet once lamented, "My people are destroyed for lack of knowledge" (Hos. 4:6). The new Christian right nonprofit organization can serve people by teaching them what God has to say about government.

## Christian Political Organizations

Prior to 1988, most religious right political activity was performed by not-for-profit 501(c)(3) and 501(c)(4) organizations.

There are many Internal Revenue Code (IRC) classifications for not-for-profit corporations, but most organizations use 501(c)(3) and 501(c)(4)s.

Such corporations may be organized and exempt from tax under certain sections of the Internal Revenue Code of 1954 and may carry on specifically defined political activities. Such corporations are exempt from tax if they adhere to guidelines set out in section 501(c)(3) of the code (charitable organizations) or section 501(c)(4) of the code (civic organizations). Examples of charitable organizations are the Boy Scouts, the Exxon Foundation, and many church or other religious organizations. Examples of civic organizations are Common Cause, Concerned Women for America, and the Eagle Forum. The 501(c)(4) category is tax exempt but contributions are not tax deductible, and therefore, the 501(c)(4) has more flexibility with regard to political activities.

In *The Law of Tax Exempt Organizations*, Bruce R. Hopkins analyzes the role of tax-exempt organizations and concludes that

> Irrespective of Toffleresque [speaking of Alvin Toffler, author of *Future Shock* and *The Third Wave*] terminology, his prognostications indicate an exciting and meaningful future, replete with a large dosage of the American tendency to create "associations." The Toffler premise suggests that nonprofit, tax-exempt organizations are an integral part of the American societal and political future.

There are several major advantages in using a tax-exempt organization for campaign projects. First, certain types of tax-exempt organizations may accept corporate donations. Second, no expenditures made by a tax-exempt organization or contributions to such organizations need be reported to the Federal Election Commission (FEC) or to your state election officials. There is one *major* rule that must be considered when you are formulating your activities for tax-exempt organizations: With the exception of political action committees, tax-exempt organizations cannot get *directly* involved in a candidate's campaign or be partisan to a candidate, political party, or specific legislation.

Tax-exempt organizations such as Moral Majority or Dr. Tim LaHaye's American Coalition for Traditional Values (ACTV) proved their worth during the eighties by registering hundreds of thousands of new evangelical voters who tend to vote for conservative Republican candidates. Moral Majority, ACTV, and Concerned Women for America have educated, registered, and motivated many traditional-values voters. The Pat Robertson campaign may have doubled or tripled the number of Christians participating in the political process.

The Rev. Lou Sheldon of Anaheim, California, has made effective use of three types of nonprofit organizations. Traditional Values Coalition [501(c)(3)], California Coalition for Traditional Values [501(c)(4)], and California Business for Traditional Values [501(c)(6)] have been very effective. This is the method for getting out the vote for the Christian right.

## Organizational Options

There are other types of tax-exempt corporations that are not subject to the provisions of federal or state elections regulations as long as they do not perform specific functions in campaigns.

Through past litigation, most areas involving political activity by 501(c)(3), 501(c)(4), or 501(c)(6) (business organizations) groups have been succinctly clarified. It is possible for such organizations to engage in nonpartisan projects that would directly benefit traditional-values, conservative causes, and free enterprise programs.

### The IRC 501(c)(3)

The IRC 501(c)(3) is a not-for-profit charitable corporation. Contributions made to a 501(c)(3) are tax deductible, but there are stringent limitations on political involvement. The 501(c)(3) can educate on issues or candidates but cannot have a political action committee (PAC) or be partisan. A 501(c)(3) organization

- cannot directly or indirectly show partiality to a political party or lobby for specific legislation.
- cannot contribute in-kind or financially to the campaign of any candidate.

The 501(c)(3) organization

- can participate in activities that are educational in character and nonpartisan. A 501(c)(3):
- can make expenditures for educational material regarding legislative issues within limitations imposed by IRC section 501(i).
- can distribute nonpartisan candidate report cards (that do not have editorial comments about the candidate).
- can produce and distribute incumbents' voting records.
- can hold educational classes pertaining to participation in the political system.
- can conduct voter registration drives.
- can do a nonpartisan get-out-the-vote telephone, radio, or literature campaign.

The 501(c)(3) charitable organization should be careful not to overvalue its tax deductible status. Internal Revenue Code limitations may confine the organization activities to the point that it can't fight the fight. Therefore, do not place funds or assets needed to win a campaign in such organizations. Keep in mind, too, that you can sell an organization's assets to a campaign for at-cost fair-market value. Some examples are:

- Selling campaign advertising space in your organization's newsletter.
- Allowing campaign information to be sent out in business mailings at the campaign's expense.
- Selling your organization's name lists.
- Doing polls or research and selling it at cost.

## How to Form a 501(c)(3)

A sample charter for forming a 501(c)(3) or 501(c)(4) or any nonprofit corporation may be obtained from your local library. Once the charter is written, a copy must be sent to your state's secretary of state. There is usually a small fee for a nonprofit filing.

A 501(c)(3) or 501(c)(4) corporation should not and cannot be formed primarily for political purposes. The corporation's activities must relate to art education, health education, public affairs, science, research, social services, humanities, or religion.

After receiving your incorporation papers, obtain and fill out the appropriate form from the Internal Revenue Service (IRS). Then send the charter and form by registered mail to the IRS to gain the tax exempt of a 501(c)(3).

The corporation may operate up to eighteen months while waiting for its official tax deductible status, but complications may arise if the IRS refuses to grant that status.

An individual may form the 501(c)(3) without legal counsel, and while this may be the most inexpensive way, it can be very costly if mistakes are made.

### Example of the Benefits of a 501(c)(3)

For a special-interest group to be effective in politics, it must be educated, motivated, organized, prepared, trained, and deployed. A 501(c)(3) nonprofit organization can effectively and legally accomplish many of those goals with corporate and individual tax deductible dollars. The following bulleted items are examples of how a 501(c)(3) organization can be involved.

### Education

The 501(c)(3) organization can
- help the general public learn how to participate in the political system.
- identify the liberal groups, such as the American Civil Liberties Union, the National Organization of Women, and the People for the American Way, and describe their objectives.
- identify conservative groups, such as Citizens Against Pornography, Concerned Women for America, the Eagle Fo-

rum, and Citizens for Excellence in Education, and describe their objectives.
- hold issue-awareness classes in churches.
- have a local radio program or produce a newsletter.
- hold nonpartisan candidate forums. All candidates must receive a letter of invitation. Be sure to keep a record of invitations sent and responses received. It would not be a bad idea to send registered letters.

## Motivation

The 501(c)(3) organization can also
- expose legislation that threatens family values and religious freedom.
- set up prayer chains or supply information to prayer groups.

## Organization/Identification

The 501(c)(3) or 501(c)(4) organization can also
- identify the Judeo-Christian traditional values of voters and workers.
- encourage study groups and prayer groups that might be politically active during a campaign.
- identify Christian activists and activist churches.
- identify Judeo-Christian pro-family officeholders.

## Training

The training a 501(c)(3) or a 501(c)(4) organization can do is limited to the knowledge and skills required for participation in the political system. Such instruction can include
- how to run for office.
- how to participate in the party system and run for party offices.
- how to produce media spots and press releases.
- how to raise funds.
- how to know the differences among political action committees, 501(c)(3) groups, 501(c)(4) groups, and others.

*Preparation*

An essential element of our political system is that a prospective voter must be registered to vote. In some states the voter must be registered as a party member to participate in that party. To help fulfill this requirement the 501(c)(3) organization can

- hold voter registration drives.
- organize car pools to get voters to the polls.
- organize phone trees in churches, prayer groups, crisis pregnancy centers, and in other 501(c)(3) organizations.

What we have outlined above is what 501(c)(3) groups can legally do. We must remember, however, to make all those assets available at a reasonable cost to Christian political action committees and 501(c)(4) groups for the actual electoral process.

# How to Form a 501(c)(4) Organization

Organizations with IRC 501(c)(4) status are referred to as civic leagues and social welfare groups. According to the IRC code, they must be established "exclusively for the promotion of social welfare," which means that they must operate primarily to bring about civic betterment and social improvement. A 501(c)(4) organization has a wide range of potential political involvement and can be more politically active than an IRC 501(c)(3) group.

An IRC 501(c)(4) organization cannot be formed for profit. Contributions made to an IRC 501(c)(4) organization do not qualify for tax-deductible charitable contribution status. One advantage, however, is that, like IRC 501(c)(3)s, corporations can contribute to the organization. Businesses may deduct their contributions under certain circumstances, if it can be shown that the contribution constitutes an ordinary and necessary expense of the business. Such contributions may be reviewed by the Internal Revenue Service.

An organization may qualify as nonprofit under Section

501(c)(4) even if it engages primarily in lobbying, as long as the lobbying is directed toward improving social welfare. Since the regulations state that social welfare activities do not include political campaigns, such an organization must devote less than half its activities to elections. Thus, an organization exempt from tax under this section may devote more than half of its activities to lobbying, and up to half of its activities to participation in political campaigns on behalf of or in opposition to candidates for public office. Of course, such activities must not violate any provision of the Federal Election Campaign Act or your local state election code.

The problems of political involvement previously discussed with respect to charitable organizations do not affect civic organizations to the same extent. Civic organizations may clearly be "conservative" or may promote a Judeo-Christian traditional-values agenda and have a purpose or purposes which may be obtained only through legislation. For instance, the Internal Revenue Service has granted exemption to organizations such as Common Cause and the Sierra Club, which have extensive legislative programs. A 501(c)(4) organization could, therefore, have a definite point of view and seek to promote that point of view through legislation and through information disseminated to the general public. Many of the activities presently carried on by political action committees, which might be inappropriate for a charitable organization, could be carried on by an organization exempt from tax under Section 501(c)(4).

## *Advantages of a 501(c)(4)*

There are many reasons for setting up a civic organization. The following list is a brief summary:

- A 501(c)(4) may receive corporate contributions.
- A 501(c)(4) is not regulated by the Federal Election Campaign Act or your local secretary of state's election code.
- A 501(c)(4) could provide for projects that the state party system, campaign budget, or political action committee couldn't.

☆　**43**　☆

*Possible Politically Oriented Activities for the*
*501(c)(4) Organization*

The 501(c)(4) organization is allowed to
- conduct local surveys, research, and polling on public policy issues.
- provide analysis of issues and election results.
- develop voter registration lists for direct mail and grassroots lobbying.
- develop strong coalitions, special interest groups, and conservative organizations through grassroots lobbying and other means.
- conduct voter registration drives
- produce and lobby for programs advocating free enterprise, less government, less government regulation, cutting government spending, and traditional-values issues.
- compare candidates by producing report cards or media ads on a wide range of key issues.
- establish and maintain a speakers' forum.
- provide and administer a college scholarship fund for high school and college students.
- target direct mail to an identified mailing list.
- initiate media campaigns to inform the public about candidates' positions on specific issues.
- organize and conduct nonpartisan get-out-the-vote phone banks on polling.
- organize training sessions on how to participate in the political process or how to organize a campaign.
- establish a volunteer recruitment and training program.
- print and mail newsletters, action alerts, and legislative alerts.
- develop computer software for grassroots activity.
- develop political training material and programs for youth.
- establish a political action committee (state or federal or both).

# How to Form a 501(c)(6) Business League

A business league is an organization made up of persons who have common business interests, which could include Christian businesses that come together to promote their common business interests. A business league cannot be organized for a profit or to provide a specific service for the members of the organization. Such an organization does not have to engage in educational, charitable, or social welfare activities.

Examples of business leagues include the United States Chamber of Commerce, the National Federation of Independent Businesses (NFIB), state and national bar associations, and various trade associations. The National Religious Broadcasters (NRB) is another example of a business league.

When mobilized, business leagues can be a formidable political force. For instance, the NRB in the state of Texas alone has over three thousand members. A business league can communicate to its membership information about political candidates that the league supports. However, a business league *cannot* communicate with the general public. This means that political statements by business leagues have to be directed *only* to members. Communications to members may include the voting record of incumbents on issues having a direct impact on business. Such communications may also include analysis of actions that hurt the interest of the leagues' members.

The best example of a business league that communicates its views on candidates is the United States Chamber of Commerce. The Chamber publishes *The Business Advocate* and distributes it to its members. This publication rates the incumbents and challengers, and informs Chamber members concerning pro-business candidates. The Chamber will only support candidates who it determines to have a 70 percent or higher "correct" voting rating.

Many business leagues are not currently expressing support for candidates. More such groups must be made aware of the candidates and their positions. They should also realize that endorsing a candidate because his or her position is in the interest of the league's members is within the limits of the law.

## Lobbying Effort

Nonprofit 501(c)(4) organizations may lobby members of Congress or state legislators.

There are two types of lobbying: *Individual*, where you as an individual may go to your state capital and visit with your legislator; and *organizational*, where you may represent a charitable organization [501(c)(3)], a civic organization [501(c)(4)], or a business league [501(c)(6)].

True lobbying is a give and take proposition. A lobbyist attempts to provide information on specific issues to legislators, present accurate information on issues to legislative committees, encourage individuals to attend committee meetings, and inform grassroots organizations about pending legislation.

Most lobbying is more effective when there is more than one person or group lobbying a legislator. Groups such as Concerned Women for America, the Eagle Forum, or Citizens for Excellence in Education might lobby along with your group. However, if you or your group are very aggressive and easily identifiable in campaigns, you may find legislators resist your message. The old adage, coined by Speaker of the House Sam Rayburn, "go along to get along," is very true in lobbying. Your legislators may have the "go along to get along" mentality, believing this is the best way to be effective in the U.S. Congress or your state house.

Your focus, then, should be on key legislation that concerns issues such as abortion, pornography, homosexuality, secular humanism, religious freedom, the family, crime, and excessive taxation.

Remember, to be an effective lobbyist, one must
- know the legislators.
- understand the legislative process (which differs some from state to state).

- get hands-on experience.
- have a sound biblical doctrine on key issues.
- focus on key legislation and know how it relates to the agendas of the liberal and conservative establishments.

## Tips on Lobbying Legislators

- Contact with a legislator should be brief, to the point, and courteous.
- Be extremely careful about threatening a legislator, such as, "We're going to defeat you at the polls if you don't vote our way." Remember, action speaks louder than words. Don't announce your plan, just do it. Once you have alienated a legislator, your effectiveness is gone.
- Don't waste time with hard-core liberals—you are not going to change their minds. Instead: pray for them and defeat them at the polls.
- Establish a rapport with the legislator's staff.
- A conversation on the stairs or coming out of committee may be your only chance to speak to legislators. Walk along with them; be brief and exact.
- Thank-you notes are important. When a legislator supports controversial or unpopular legislation for you, thank him or her and have your friends do so. Thank legislators, too, for seeing you or reviewing your written material.

## Examples of Effective Lobbying Techniques

Lobbying is a technique that usually takes the personality of biblical models like Joseph, Obadiah, Esther, or Daniel. Follow their examples and never compromise the Word of God to obtain victory. If you do, it will be a hollow victory. Judas is a prime example of one who thought compromise with the Pharisees would save the kingdom.

Campaigns that elect conservative candidates and expose liberal candidates for what they are will help ensure effective lobbying. In ten years of lobbying, Christians have not overturned abortion, effectively thwarted homosexual activism, or turned the tide of secular humanism. It takes victory at the polls to have true victory at the legislative level.

Senator Bentsen from Texas put it succinctly during Judge Bork's Supreme Court nomination hearings. According to the *Dallas Morning News* in 1987, Bentsen stated that all the letters and phone calls in Bork's support were not as important as votes in November. So with his mail and phone calls running fifty to one for Bork, he voted to turn Bork down. Had he believed those phone calls represented active voters, he would have voted differently.

## Adopt-a-Legislator

You may want to create a program in your state capital modeled after that of Barbara Plating of the American Coalition for Life: the "Adopt-a-Congressman" program in Washington. Adopt-a-legislator programs are usually located in the state capital. Volunteers from around the capital form a committee to visit the legislator on a regular basis, usually once a week.

To form such a program call Christian activists that live not more than an hour's drive from the capital. Try to assign at least one activist to every four legislators.

Duties of activists include visiting assigned legislators at least once a week and attending committee meetings regarding key issues. Volunteers could schedule breakfast, lunch, or late afternoon visits, always at the legislator's convenience. Visits can include an exchange of information on issues and legislation and prayer time.

When appropriate, activists should contact people that live in the legislator's district. Send them a legislative alert describing pending pro-family legislation and encourage them to call or write their legislators, urging them to vote in favor.

☆ **48** ☆

## The Effective Use of a Nonprofit 501(c)(4) Organization: An Example

In April of 1989, a special congressional election was held in Wyoming to fill the seat left by Congressman Dick Chenney's appointment as secretary of defense.

The two major candidates were State Senator John Vinich and State Representative Craig Thomas. Vinich was a thirty-eight-year-old liberal who had run unsuccessfully in the fall of 1988 against a strong conservative incumbent, Senator Malcolm Wallop. Vinich lost, but by only 1.5 percent of the vote.

During his campaign against Wallop, Vinich had trouble with pro-life people, and so April 6, 1989, he sent a letter to all the Catholic priests in Wyoming stating that he was personally against abortion but "did not know what to do about a woman's private choice to have an abortion." Perhaps Vinich hoped that statement would win over the pro-life, pro-family activists.

Craig Thomas had served twelve years as state representative from Natrona County, one of the largest counties in Wyoming. But Representative Thomas did not have statewide name recognition. He did, however, have a conservative platform and a voting record almost the exact opposite of Vinich's.

The Good Government Group (GGG), a local conservative political organization, used a polling and research service out of California to send questionnaires to all the candidates, two of whom weren't really in the running, Don Johnson, a white supremacist running as an independent, and Craig McCurre, running as the Libertarian party candidate. McCurre would be a problem to the GGG effort, because many home schoolers and charismatics were leaning toward McCurre. Unfortunately, those home schoolers and charismatics had not done enough research on his positions or his party's platform, which reflected antitraditional values. For example, McCurre was for the legalization of drugs.

The GGG had visited with many people in the pro-family community around the state but began its work with only thirty-

# PRO-FAMILY VOTER REPORT CARD

|  | Vinich | Thomas | Pro-Family |
|---|---|---|---|
| **Crime** | | | |
| 1. Provide for a 3-year imprisonment for any prisoner escaping from a county jail. | Oppose | Support | Support |
| 2. Allow a judge to determine whether criminals should be in county jails or prisons. This would help overcrowding. | Oppose | Support | Support |
| 3. Increase the number of penitentiaries. | Oppose | Support | Support |
| 4. Provide a surcharge on fines for any person convicted of driving under the influence of liquor. | Oppose | Support | Support |
| 5. Legalize gambling and the lottery. | Support | Oppose | Oppose |
| **Drug & Substance Abuse** | | | |
| 1. Federal law legalizing marijuana. | *RTA | Oppose | Oppose |
| 2. Strengthen penalities and procedures for testing drivers under the influence of alcohol. | Oppose | Support | Support |
| **Family Values** | | | |
| 1. Overturn Roe vs. Wade. | Oppose | Support | Support |
| 2. Provide birth control contraceptive services and devices to minors in public schools. | Support | Oppose | Oppose |
| 3. Pass the Equal Rights Amendment. | Support | Oppose | Oppose |
| 4. Abortion on demand. | Support | Oppose | Oppose |
| **Economics** | | | |
| 1. Balance budget amendment. | Oppose | Support | Support |
| 2. Right to Work. | Oppose | Support | Support |

Special Congressional Election is Wednesday, April 26

(This is an educational nonpartisan paper comparing the two leading candidates' positions on pro-family values. This is not an endorsement of any candidate or party. The above information was taken from interviews, newspaper reports, and surveys sent to each candidate.)

---

*RTA: Refused to Answer

eight hard-core Christian activist committees. Its purpose was to educate the conservative electorate on the candidates' positions.

McCurre and Vinich refused to answer the questionnaire. Thomas sent back his questionnaire, giving him a 90 percent pro-family rating.

By the time I arrived in Wyoming to aid the efforts of the GGG, a mud-slinging campaign was in progress, and Thomas was trailing by twelve to fifteen points in the polls.

In an effort to change the public's perception of the candidates, we researched Thomas' and Vinich's voting records in the categories of crime, family values, economics, and substance abuse. In all areas, Vinich was the ideological opposite of Thomas. We then designed pro-family voter report cards to focus on candidates' positions and to compare them to a pro-family orientation.

When preparing a questionnaire, be sure the questions are clear and not one-sided. The key is simplicity. Send your questionnaires by fax or registered mail. Keep a record of completed questionnaires that you receive. Follow up those that have not been sent back with a call. If the answers don't agree with the statements or position papers by candidates, you may use their statements or position papers by documenting your source. Make your report card easy to read and understand. Never, never twist answers to give advantage to your candidate. If you are 501(c)(4) or 501(c)(3), this makes the piece an activist piece, which is illegal.

Concerning family values, we learned that saying pro-life or pro-choice isn't enough. So we included some of Vinich's own statements such as: "I personally oppose abortion, but I believe it should be left to a woman and her doctor."

We also began to recruit leaders for each city in every county. We had a phone bank calling Christian activists and former Pat Robertson supporters to see if they favored Vinich or Thomas. Those that favored Thomas were recruited as volunteers to work in the church or community.

In addition, we set up radio ads and printed a hundred thousand pieces of literature, mailing them to a thousand churches throughout the state, made a book documenting all the answers used in the pro-family voter report card, and recruited youth teams in ten counties to work on Saturday to put report cards on car windows in shopping malls and to go house to house.

We also encouraged a group of citizens to pay for and distribute a thousand 8½ by 17 posters supporting Thomas as the pro-family candidate. Because of its IRC status, the Good Government Group could not print or distribute any material that was partisan, but we could encourage others to do so.

We sent documentation for our report cards to all the leaders and churches that were going to distribute the report card, and we distributed one hundred thousand report cards to six hundred churches.

The Vinich campaign denounced our report card as fiction, so we faxed proof of our report card to the major newspapers, the TV stations, and the Associated Press. Media stories then were changed to reflect that the Good Government Group could substantiate their report card.

Wyoming's secretary of state (who was pro-Vinich) called us to ask if we were a political action committee. We informed them we were an education group with 501(c)(4) status.

*Results:* Vinich went down eight to ten points in the polls. We were supported by nonpartisan phone banks using church groups, prayer groups, individuals, and crisis pregnancy volunteers. Craig Thomas won the race with 53 percent of the vote.

How much credit should GGG and the pro-family movement be given? That can be left to opinion. Beyond dispute is the fact that we took action to educate those in the church and special-interest groups and encourage them to vote.

## The Twenty-First Century

The twenty-first century is only ten critical years away. I believe it's safe to speculate that the nation's baby boomers' primary interest will soon be family and security. That age group has been turning to the church in increasing numbers. They will be the new conservatives of the twenty-first century. Having gone through the failure of the values-clarification philosophy of secular humanists, these new conservatives recognize that the world can be changed only by belief in God and godly principles.

The baby boomers are recognizing the "big lie" (that God is dead and that man is capable of solving his own problems alone), and they are presently searching for the truth. Through television evangelism, the Jesus movement, the charismatic movement, and now through an awakening in mainline denominations, baby boomers are finding Jesus Christ to be the "Truth and the Light." This will certainly influence the present political and social structure of America.

It has been forty-five years since a major world war. The United States has not experienced a totally crippling financial crisis since 1929. We have experienced a revolution in technology and information systems. Our standard of living rates among the highest in the world. Yet, why is there such a sense that something is extremely wrong? Could it be that the generation of baby boomers recognizes, just as John warns us in Revelation 21, that we must "return to our first love"?

You and other like-minded people reading this book may be a part of the remnant that hears God's call and is willing to return this nation to its dependence on God. The call is for America to believe in biblical principles, the foundation our government was built upon. Your personal vision for America and the willingness to act on that vision may help preserve this republic.

The technology is available today to make grassroots America effective in politics again. Special elections or elections with traditional low voter turnouts can be the opportunity to make dynamic changes, putting control back in the hands of the common citizen. To be effective we must be able to accomplish certain tasks:

- Identify like-minded voters.
- Obtain and retain permanent data on voters.
- Communicate efficiently and economically with voters.

- Track voting trends of the electorate.
- Know the voting record of incumbents.
- Organize from the precinct level to the congressional districts.

There are over an estimated sixty million born-again Christians in America. We are a people of strong traditions and strong family units, and we are hospitable and generous. We are located in every area of society. The born-again experience transcends other loyalties and makes us a very *special* special-interest group. With God's help, we can redeem the American political system.

# Political Action Committees

Political action committees,[1] or PACs as they are usually referred to, were created by politicians and are often used as a mechanism to help incumbents stay in office. When used effectively, a PAC may be the best vehicle to effect the election of any candidate.

## Why Form a PAC?

There are at least four good reasons why forming a PAC is helpful.

1. A PAC is the legal way a special-interest group can be involved in a campaign.

2. Why not give the money your group raises to candidates of your choice? Under law, PACs can do this.

3. A five- or twenty-dollar contribution from an individual does not get the same attention from the candidate as a five-hundred- or one-thousand-dollar PAC donation.

4. Your group can pool its resources to help a candidate, and

---

1. If you are planning to start a federal or state PAC, use the information in this book only for general knowledge. You should contact the Federal Elections Commission or State Election official and obtain the official campaign guide for separate segregated PACs and for nonconnected PACs.

when the campaign is over you can retain assets such as name lists, voter data, and donor information.

## Purpose for PAC Activities

PAC activities have a variety of short and long-term goals. Some of those goals are as follows:

To research state races and compare the Judeo-Christian work force and voting strength of moderate Republicans with those who vote in Republican primaries.

To build a coalition using those numbers, which will give a projection of where favorable people may be elected.

To compile data on each candidate.

To analyze the voting trend of the past eight years in each targeted area.

To compile numbers of the Judeo-Christian voting strength in each targeted area.

Most state and local races have no limit on the amount of funds that can be donated or spent by individuals or PACs. Your PAC may decide to raise funds to spend on a statewide race; and then make any remaining funds available to other races that seem promising.

For example, you can raise funds and coordinate a statewide voter registration drive in targeted areas under the activity of a U.S. Senate race. Then those newly registered voters will be identified for access during other worthwhile races.

Special radio and TV ads for high profile races and other designated races should be aired the last two weeks of a campaign. Those ads would run on rural cable, radio, and all Christian radio and TV stations. Such ads can cost as little as fifteen dollars for a sixty-second spot. Generally, the ad will air on Sundays and late at night. Schedule them along with programs that appeal to your voters.

Use automatic dialing machines for designated state representative races and to help get out the vote for local candidates.

Use local voter report cards as well as state and national report cards to inform voters on the candidates' positions. These report cards can be more partisan.

Do educational programs in the high minority and rural areas to make voters aware of the Democratic and Republican platforms. Reproduce any gay rights articles supporting the Democratic party and candidates and distribute them. Concentrate your educational efforts on issues such as AIDS, taxes, spending, and crime.

Tactics like those will surely help elect more Judeo-Christian officials.

## Types of PACs

PACs have a IRC 501(c)(5) classification. They are not-for-profit, tax-exempt organizations, but donations to them are not tax deductible.

There are two major categories of PACs: *federal* and *state*. Either type of PAC is fairly simple to organize. All you need are the forms from the Federal Election Commission in Washington, D.C., for a federal PAC and/or forms from the secretary of state in your state for a state PAC. You will need a person to be the treasurer and he or she will sign the forms and be responsible for making a financial report to the appropriate federal or state agency. That agency will send forms for the treasurer to fill out. The form requests information in two categories: *expenditures* and *receipts*. The treasurer will list all expenditures during a given time period and list all receipts for the same period.

The same name can be used for a federal or state PAC by simply filling out the forms for each. If you do this, however, remember never to commingle the funds. Always have two separate bank accounts, two bookkeeping systems, and separate files. One advantage for having one committee name for both types of PACs is the increased name familiarity.

Should you have more than one PAC? You will find the professionals have many PACs, and there are good reasons for creating multiple PACs.

- PACs can donate to PACs.
- You may wish to reach different special-interest groups with different PACs.
- You may wish to support different candidates with different PACs.
- You may want a PAC connected to a candidate, while another PAC is not.
- Each PAC has an allowable amount it can contribute to a candidate. Having more than one PAC may increase the funds given to a candidate.

## The Federal PAC

If you are going to help finance a candidate running for the U.S. Senate, the U.S. House of Representatives, or President, then the committee must register with the Federal Election Commission. The committee can directly spend on or contribute to a federal candidate up to five thousand dollars. The federal PAC can also contribute up to ten thousand dollars in a calendar year to another fund. (Please check for current regulations; these change yearly.)

There are some interesting advantages to the federal PAC. A federal PAC can only spend directly or contribute directly five thousand dollars to its favorite candidate, but the PAC can also spend up to five thousand dollars for each opposing candidate. Your committee can have mailings, radio programs, billboards, TV ads, and so forth explaining why opposing candidates should not be elected. Thus, if there are six Republicans and six Democrats in the race, your PAC could spend sixty thousand dollars.

## Types of Federal PACs

A *connected* PAC is in contact with or in association with a federal candidate. A *nonconnected* PAC can do brochures, signs, and media advertising without consultation with the federal candidate or his or her staff. This is called *nonauthorized activity*, and a disclaimer must be in all materials and advertisements.

## Nonconnected PACs[2]

1. A nonconnected political action committee does not have a "connected organization," that is, it is not connected to (or sponsored by) a corporation or labor organization. Such a committee is formed by an individual or groups of individuals.

2. A nonconnected PAC must itself pay for all the day-to-day costs of running the committee, using the contributions it raises.

3. A nonconnected committee may solicit any individual, group, or committee for contributions.

4. A nonconnected group becomes a political action committee under the Federal Election Campaign Act when it receives contributions or makes expenditures exceeding one thousand dollars per calendar year. The committee must register as a political action committee within ten days of exceeding the one-thousand-dollar threshold.

5. A nonconnected PAC may donate five thousand dollars to any candidate, spend five thousand dollars for each opposing candidate, and donate ten thousand dollars to another political action committee annually.

While nonconnected PACs need to be careful about contact with a candidate or his or her staff, don't feel you can't even communicate with the candidate to find out his or her positions on issues. But don't get overly enthusiastic. If a nonconnected committee asks the candidate what it can do to help, that would make its efforts and expenditure an in-kind contribution. That is allowable only if your committee has not reached the maximum monetary donation allowable to the candidate.

According to FEC regulations, you cannot call individuals or

---

2. Information in this section has been taken from the Federal Election Regulation Code (Washington, D.C., 1988 edition).

committees and tell them not to do certain projects, such as independent ads or the gathering of names on petitions.

Any expenditures to finance the distribution or reprinting of campaign materials or media ads *prepared by a candidate's campaign* are not independent expenditures. An independent expenditure is any expenditure made on behalf of a candidate without the knowledge of the candidate's campaign staff. Therefore, you must create your own yard signs, brochures, or media ads for such materials to be considered independent. Sometimes this works best if you want to show a candidate's position on traditional values and pro-family issues.

If a political committee hires a *former employee of a candidate's campaign,* any expenditures made by that committee on behalf of the candidate or in opposition to the opponent is presumed *not* to be independent.

If a nonconnected committee and a candidate that the committee has spent money on uses *the same consultant or vendor,* the expenditure is not an independent expenditure. You need to be careful not to pay a consultant or even talk with a consultant that your candidate also uses.

An expenditure by a nonconnected committee to solicit the public for contributions to a candidate is not independent if *the committee actually collects and forwards the contributions* to the candidate's committee. You may invite a candidate or candidates to speak at a fund-raising forum or rally, and the funds spent or raised are independent if you do not forward them to the candidate's committee.

For example, if the Coalition of Politically Active Christians (COPAC) decides to purchase a newspaper ad for a candidate after talking to the candidate and his or her staff, the ad would not qualify as independent. If the committee wanted to produce a poster or brochure but use slogans written by the candidate's committee, the expenditure would not be independent. If your committee contacts the candidate about an idea or the need for such material, the ad or brochure must carry a disclaimer saying it was *authorized by the candidate* such as, *Paid for by COPAC and authorized by the John Smith-for-Senate Committee.*

As long as your committee does not communicate with the candidate's committee, the expenditure may qualify as an *independent expenditure.* When supporting a candidate directly for office with brochures, billboards, leaflets, media ads, the committee must use a disclaimer saying it was *not authorized by the candidate or candidate's staff* such as, *Paid for by COPAC and not authorized by any candidate or candidate's committee.*

Your nonconnected political committee may make up to a five-thousand-dollar annual contribution to as many other committees as it wishes. This is in addition to the two thousand dollars spent or given in-kind to a candidate's committee.

In some states, funds donated by your PAC to an office account to support the officeholder's activities, but not the campaign, of a federal or state officeholder are not considered campaign contributions or expenditures even if the officeholder is a candidate for federal office. An example would be money used to help pay for office staff. Such expenditures must not be made for the purpose of influencing a federal election.

Your committee may use money for voter education, voter registration, get-out-the-vote drives, and so forth without those expenses being considered in-kind contributions. All such materials must be nonpartisan and neither for nor against a federal candidate.

## Contributions

- *Total contributed on an annual basis.* A committee may receive up to five thousand dollars from an individual. A corporation cannot contribute to a PAC.
- *Husband and wife.* A check for ten thousand dollars from a joint account must have both signatures.
- *Identifying contributions.* For contributions exceeding

fifty dollars, the record must show the date received and the donor's name and address.

- *Contributions aggregating over two hundred dollars.* For contributions annually aggregating over two hundred dollars, the committee records must identify the donor by name, the date each donation is received, the donor's occupation, and the name of his or her employer.

- *Contributions from other political committees.* Your committee's records must identify all contributions by other political committees—regardless of the amount—by amount, date received, and name and address of the contributing committee.

- *Earmarking and contribution limits.* An earmarked or designated contribution may be passed through to a candidate without being aggregated against the PAC limits. The PAC must not exercise control over the choice of the intended recipient of the contribution. This earmarked contribution must be forwarded within ten days to its designated recipient.

## Recording Disbursement

- *Petty cash.* A written record of petty cash disbursement must be kept if a petty cash fund is maintained. Payments from petty cash to one person for any one purchase or transaction may not exceed one hundred dollars.

- *Disbursement exceeding two hundred dollars.* For each single disbursement that exceeds two hundred dollars, the committee must also keep a receipt, invoice, and a cancelled check. Be sure to write on the check what the check was for.

Transfers of funds to affiliated committees must be itemized regardless of the amount.

Monetary and in-kind contributions made to candidate committees and other political committees must be itemized regardless of the amount.

## Independent Expenditures

A committee must report the total amount of its independent expenditures and itemize those exceeding or aggregating over two hundred dollars per calendar year.

A nonconnected political committee may be sponsored by an organization, that is, a partnership or some other semi-incorporated group. The sponsoring organization may make in-kind or direct contributions not to exceed five thousand dollars per calendar year.

A sponsoring organization may provide free legal and accounting services to a nonconnected committee if the services are provided solely to help the committee comply with federal election campaign law and if individuals performing the services are the regular employees of the organization. Such support does not count toward the five-thousand-dollar limitation. Accounting

## FEDERAL ELECTION CAMPAIGN CONTRIBUTION GUIDE

|  | To Candidate or Authorized Committee | To National Party PCY** | Other Committee PCY |
|---|---|---|---|
| Contributions from individual | $1,000/election | $20,000 | $5,000 |
| Multicandidate* Committee | 5,000 | 20,000 | 5,000 |
| Party Committee | 1,000 or 5,000/election | No limit | 5,000 |
| Republican or Democratic, Senatorial, Congressional | 17,500 | — | — |
| Any Other Committee | 1,000/election | 20,000 | 5,000 |

*nonconnected committees or "multicandidate" and any other committee
**per calendar year

services may be donated by an accounting firm as long as the service concerns compliance with federal election campaign laws.

## A Segregated Committee

A 501(c)(4) or 501(c)(6) organization may form a political action committee. This committee must not be under the direct control of the parent organization or corporation.

1. A separate segregated fund (SSF) is always connected to an organization and, by definition, designates the existence of a political action committee.

2. The connected organization with an SSF is prohibited from making any contributions or expenditures in connection with a federal election campaign that directly helps a candidate.

3. As soon as a tax-exempt organization establishes an SSF, the organization must register its PAC within ten days after that date.

4. The 501(c)(4) or 501(c)(6) organization is forbidden from making direct contributions to a candidate or party. Therefore, all separate segregated funds must be kept in a separate bank account.

5. On the statement of organization, the PAC that controls an SSF must list the name and address of its connected organization.

6. A corporation 501(c)(5) and 501(c)(6) may form more than one PAC, but the statement of organization must list all affiliated PACs.

7. A connected organization may use its treasury money to pay for costs incurred in setting up and maintaining the SSF. Treasury money may be used to pay for office space, phones, salaries, utilities, supplies, bank charges, legal fees, and accounting costs.

A connected organization may also use its treasury funds to pay for the costs of soliciting contributions to the SSF and for certain costs of other fund-raising activities. If an SSF pays any expenses that could be paid by the connected organization, the organization may reimburse the SSF but must do so within thirty days.

8. The PAC controlling an SSF may solicit its noncorporate members and families.

- A membership organization may solicit its own executives and administrative personnel.
- Dues or membership fees cannot be placed in the SSF.

9. All contributions to a candidate from an SSF must follow the same limits and restrictions as contributions from a nonconnected committee.

10. If the SSF's sponsoring organization advocates the election of more than one candidate, the PAC controlling the SSF should distribute its resources and campaign efforts equally to all the candidates. There is a reporting limit of two thousand dollars per candidate.

11. Activities that are not considered in-kind contributions to a candidate's campaign include informing voters of the voting records of incumbents, distributing nonpartisan voter report cards and making the results public, encouraging voter registration, and holding candidate debates.

Nonpartisan voter report cards produced with monies from an SSF need to follow specific guidelines:

- Questions must be directed to all candidates.
- Voter guides should reprint verbal responses without changes.
- Wording of the questions should not favor any position on the issues.
- The voter report card should exclude any editorial position on the issues.

Those rules do not apply to a report card produced by a nonpartisan tax-exempt organization.

Voter registration drives and voter information programs may be made possible by an SSF without financial expenditure limits.

## Independent Expenditures

In addition to contributing to candidates, a PAC may support or oppose candidates by making independent expenditures. Independent expenditures are not considered contributions, and therefore, do not count against the maximum contribution limits. However, contributions to a committee making independent expenditures are subject to the limits. The following is an overview; the federal regulations will need to be consulted for complete information.

An independent expenditure is an expenditure for a communication expressly advocating the election or defeat of a clearly identified candidate that is *NOT made with the cooperation or prior consent of, or in consultation with, or at the request or suggestion of* any candidate's campaign.

Any expenditure made in cooperation, consultation, or in concert with the candidate's campaign or as a result of the campaign's request or suggestion is considered an in-kind contribution, not an independent expenditure.

## The State PAC

Each state's regulations will vary somewhat with regard to the amount of contribution that a PAC can make to a state or local candidate. The length of time a PAC must be in existence before it can make a contribution to a candidate will be determined by your state's secretary of state. You should contact your secretary of state or state election commission and obtain a copy of the rules and regulations to help answer any questions.

Why form state PACs? Legally, they are the safest vehicle for political activity. They also are apt to receive media attention and be in a position to influence political parties and platforms.

You will also find that state PACs are an excellent way to utilize money to defeat an unfavorable candidate. In most states donations to PACs of less than one hundred dollars can be combined and not reported individually.

## A State PAC's Different Functions

Your PAC may want to work in a simplified form and only for a specific period of time. Your only goal may be to raise funds for a candidate and help inform the Judeo-Christian community of the candidate's stand on traditional values. In addition, your PAC may also decide to raise funds, print material, and make yard signs or political advertisements.

A PAC fund may come from people you associate with, such as prayer groups, individuals, and special interest groups wanting more involvement in a campaign but not under the authority of a certain candidate. To do this your PAC may want to work for several candidates by setting up phone banks, recruiting volunteers to conduct polls, going door-to-door to inform people about the candidates, or presenting your issues through the media.

Two types of state PACs are *general purpose* and *specific purpose*. You'll want to get a copy of your state's regulations on political action committees in order to be in total compliance.

### General Purpose PAC

A general purpose PAC is one having among its principal functions the acceptance of contributions or the making of expenditures

- to support or oppose candidates or offices that have not yet been specified.

- to support or oppose legislation that is not yet specifically identified.

- to assist as yet unspecified office holders with their nonreimbursable expenses in connection with the performance of their duties of office.

The general purpose PAC, then, can receive contributions to be used at a later date to promote the aims and vision of the PAC.

The general purpose committee in most states allows for a broad range of activity so that it may be able to support more than one candidate or legislative issue.

## Specific Purpose PAC

The specific purpose PAC differs from the general purpose PAC in that it:

- Supports or opposes specifically listed candidates.
- Supports legislation listed on your organization's report.
- Assists specifically designated office holders with their non-reimbursable expenses in connection with the performance of their duties of office.

An example of a specific purpose PAC would be a group of people who come together for the specific purpose of accepting contributions and/or making expenditures in support of or in opposition to a specific candidate or race, such as city council or lieutenant governor

## General Guidelines for State PACs

A *contribution* usually is defined and qualified in the following ways:

- A contribution is any advance, loan, deposit, or transfer of funds, goods, services, or any other thing of value, or any contract or obligation to a candidate for office or to an officeholder.
- In most states, it is unlawful for a person other than a general purpose PAC to accept a single contribution from a person in the form of *cash* that exceeds one hundred dollars.
- A committee must be organized prior to an election or to making contributions within the time limitation given by the state.
- In most states, an individual may donate his or her own personal services and personal traveling expenses to aid or defeat any candidate or measure, if he or she is not compensated or reimbursed.

Your PAC can do much more work than a tax-exempt 501(c)(4) or 501(c)(6) organization. Since the PAC is created for direct political action in support of or opposition to a candidate, it is the ideal vehicle.

You might want to start by forming a state general purpose PAC and get involved in your state and local elections. If you do create a federal PAC, be sure you have a copy of the regulations and keep all funds and records separate from those of your state PAC.

### Caution

Do not try to do with a tax-exempt or nonprofit organization what it can't legally do. Be sure to get the regulations from your state and federal government. You may also want to go to your library to see if it has any books on PACs.

The treasurer of a PAC has the power to dismantle a PAC, spend money, or create bills. He or she is personally responsible for all debt. In selecting a treasurer or governing board, it would be good to use the same criteria Paul told Timothy to use in selecting elders or deacons, except I'm not suggesting you eliminate women from participating as treasurer. Character, morality, and integrity are more important than gender.

## Types of Function

A PAC can function in two ways: as a political data action center or as an organization.

### Political Data Action Center

This type of a PAC usually does not field candidates or have members, but instead is a service to pro-family traditional-values candidates by

- developing a computer data bank of voters' names, analyzing that data for voting trends, volunteer activity, minority status, and financial contributions.
- networking with churches, organizations, and existing groups to supply volunteers to conduct voter registration drives.
- Researching candidate's positions, researching office-holder's voting records, and producing candidate report cards.

- getting out the vote (GOTV) campaigns using automatic dialing equipment and phone banks.
- providing financial contributions to candidates and providing funds to existing organizations for research, GOTV, and registration.

## Developing a PAC Organization

If you are going to develop a PAC as an organization, then you should file as a state PAC. That will give you more flexibility. The state PAC organization then can form a federal PAC to work only on federal campaigns. Remember to keep separate accounts. Usually assets helping a federal candidate are counted as an independent contribution or an in-kind contribution. Check the federal regulations regarding the use of office equipment and other items that may not be charged to a campaign.

The basic purpose of your PAC is to develop a network of volunteers and a plan of action for utilizing the money, material, and volunteers for the benefit of various conservative candidates. A PAC organization may field its own candidates. It can also aid the existing staff and campaign efforts of candidates that embrace Judeo-Christian traditional values and help lobby officeholders on pro-family issues.

The local PAC organization's initial objective is to identify the conservative constituency and learn its needs, concerns, and location.

How can you do this?

- Determine how many volunteers might become involved in a given campaign; determine who the leadership is or develop new leadership.
- Develop a local steering committee comprising businessmen, pastors, and civic leaders to recommend ways to increase the total effectiveness of the conservative Judeo-Christian involvement in politics.
- Identify the alliances of the conservative Judeo-Christian community with other community organizations.

The conservative, traditional-values voters must become organized so that a bloc vote can change our government by directly selecting people to hold all levels of office, from council member to congressional representative.

Two essential aspects of the PAC are (1) establishing a network of traditional-values volunteers and (2) identifying conservative voters. No area of the community should be excluded. It is important to avoid labeling an individual or ethnic group Democrat or Republican; rather, a line of communication should be established with all potential voters.

The membership application form (or volunteer form during an actual campaign) is a key item and should be a focal point of activity during the early stages of growth and organization. A committee should be assigned and headed up by a volunteer coordinator or membership chairman to secure as many completed volunteer and member forms as possible. Completed forms should be processed as quickly as possible in order to assign members to activities in areas of their interest and organize precinct groups, church awareness groups, and voting area groups.

The most effective means of getting volunteers is to personally ask friends, church members, or groups. A volunteer phone bank can call each person on church and Christian organization lists from an office or home. Remember to let people and groups be involved where their hearts are and not force them to support a candidate they do not believe in.

## Leave Moderation to the Candidate and the Party

Success in a political or legislative battle may require the building of a coalition. Be sure that you are not asking people to compromise moral principles in order to build a winning alliance. However, do not sacrifice God's principles on the altar of man's traditions.

Your PAC represents the constitutional Judeo-Christian and biblical traditional values this country was founded on, not personal or denominational doctrine. It will be a Judeo-Christian voice that cannot be denied or moderated. Stand where you must stand. It is important that the PAC's steering committee be in a majority agreement concerning alliance and candidates.

## Steps to Building a Christian PAC

To be successful, a Christian PAC depends on the acceptance and cooperation of the Christian community. Therefore:
- Start with an election or event that has widespread Christian community support.
- Visit with local area pastors to enlist their support.
- Recruit coordinators for each church.
- Build a church awareness program first as a 501(c)(4) organization and then set up your PAC. There are four reasons why you should build a church awareness program first: (1) churches are the center of influence in the Christian community; (2) meeting times or venues do not have to be created because Christians meet each week; (3) numerous resources are available—buildings, people, and financial contributors; and (4) members of a church may represent most areas of a town.

### Logistical Needs for an Effective Christian PAC

For a PAC to be effective, some of the logistical needs are
- up to a 20 megabyte IBM compatible computer, preferably with modem.
- at least one automatic dialing machine.
- files organized by districts, areas, and precincts.
- maps of counties with precincts.
- a precinct map log by streets, obtainable from the local election administration.
- legal formation of a state and/or federal PAC.
- federal PAC forms, which may be obtained by writing to the Federal Election Commission, Washington, DC, or by

calling 1-800-424-9530. A federal PAC is required to raise funds and to contribute jointly to a congressman, U.S. senator, and the presidential campaign.

- state PAC forms, which are available from your state capital and the secretary of state. The state PAC may have the same name as the federal PAC, but separate financial records must be maintained.

# Mobilizing the Christian PAC

If Christians can be mobilized, they have the opportunity of affecting the political agenda of Congress in the twenty-first century. There is an excellent chance for Christian traditional-values voters to comprise over 50 percent of the delegates at some of the state and national political conventions in the coming years.

This chapter should help you with proven methodologies for almost everything that needs to be done. Full-time personnel, people dedicated to lead, are essential. Your local program will grow much faster if you have a full-time or part-time staffer.

**Objectives to work toward at the state level.** A full-time worker at the state level could help bring together a coalition of Christian activist organizations and their leaders. Your PAC should be part of that coalition.

The state director could also moderate a forum of all the conservative organizations within the state, thus enabling Christians to give leadership to the state's conservative movement.

The state full-time worker could function as executive director of the state coalition, lobbyist for member organizations desiring to be represented, moderator of the conservative forum, and supervisor of the full-time district workers.

Objectives to work toward at the state senatorial district level. A director should be named for each state senatorial district in the state. The senatorial district director organizes the district by executing a proven plan to:

- identify the Judeo-Christian traditional-values voters and activate the conservative voters in the district by precinct, which will aid in establishing a county organization.
- recruit a coordinator for each county commissioner district or designated voting area.
- meet with key pastors in each congressional district or county and form a pastor's coalition.
- train Christians through local churches and neighborhood groups on political involvement and issues.
- work with other district directors to implement prayer groups, coordinate lobbying efforts, and to encourage financial giving, voter registration, and turn-out-the-vote efforts.

## Nehemiah: A Biblical Standard for Leadership

Building a strong Christian political organization demands the qualities of a Nehemiah, one who seeks God's counsel, moves with authority, has access to assets, is able to impart a vision to the people, attracts people willing to do their part, does not listen to doubt, is able to overcome adversity, and has the tenacity to finish the job (see Neh. 1—6).

God is a God of order and purpose. The leaders of your PAC must find and follow the scriptural purposes of God in order to move in His authority and blessing. That can only be done through much prayer.

### Nehemiah's Leadership Characteristics

The leaders that build a PAC should have the characteristics of Nehemiah.

**Nehemiah sought God's counsel** (see Neh. 1:5). The leaders

## INTEREST INVENTORY

Name _____

Address _____ Precinct _____

City _____ State _____ Zip _____

Home Phone _____ Work Phone _____

Church _____

Please provide me with more information in order that I may participate in the following activities:

☐ A church issues awareness group.

☐ A neighborhood program for prayer or analyzing issues.

☐ Contacting my elected officials on issues of interest to me.

☐ The political party caucus and convention process.

☐ Participate in a campaign.

☐ Telephoning voters concerning issues or candidates.

☐ Clerical duties for issues or candidates.

☐ Neighborhood literature distribution about issues or candidates.

☐ Becoming a contact person for my church.

☐ Being informed of Christian candidates and activist organizations needing financial support.

of a PAC must know their counsel comes from the Lord God.

**Nehemiah obtained proper permission to do the task** (see Neh. 2:5). We must have the permission from the proper authorities—God and human—in order to begin the work righteously. There must be accountability for the assets and authority entrusted to PAC leadership.

**Nehemiah obtained the assets to do the task** (see Neh. 2:7). We cannot accomplish a task or build a PAC without the proper assets available to us. You should not assume that just because the task is noble or righteous the keepers of His assets will turn those assets over to you without first determining your intentions.

Nehemiah knew the proper time to declare God's plan (see Neh. 2:12). As one builds a political organization, one must know when and with whom to share planning. Speaking too quickly and to the wrong person could jeopardize the work.

Nehemiah reconnoitered the situation (see Neh. 2:13). Before declaring plans to the people, study the task to know what is needed to complete the task.

Nehemiah knew he must be able to impart God's vision to the people (see Neh. 2:17). The leadership of a PAC must be able to share God's vision of government to the people in an understandable way.

Nehemiah knew the people must be able to recognize that he was under both God's and the king's authority (see Neh. 2:18). The people must be willing to yield to such leadership.

Nehemiah managed his assets and had them available to the workers (see Neh. 2:20). The PAC members assigned to logistics, printing, signs, shipping, and so forth must realize volunteers cannot work without material and a political army cannot be effective without a supply line.

Nehemiah enlisted leaders who had a heart for God (see Neh. 2:20). The PAC campaign chairperson, and other leaders, must have a heart for God.

Nehemiah didn't forsake the vision when others mocked him (see Neh. 4:1). When you begin to accomplish a goal threatening the established political order, you will find those who will mock you. You must fix your eyes toward victory and not look back. Bible believers should not be embarrassed nor shirk the responsibility of applying biblical absolutes and moral standards to government.

## Governor's Race in the 1990 Texas Primary

Your 501(c)(4) and political action committee working as a one-two punch can have a major effect on the outcome of a primary election.

One example is the proper usage of a 501(c)(4) (an asset gathering organization, i.e., names, research, money) and a political action committee (an asset using organization). Most 501(c)(3)s and 501(c)(4)s have their assets in such a position that they are no longer usable in an activism campaign. The 1990 primary in Texas was a prime example of this.

There were two primary candidates that took a pro-life/pro-family position: Texas railroad commissioner Kent Hance and Texas businessman Clayton Williams. Hance ran for governor of Texas in 1986 and lost but was later appointed Texas railroad commissioner. Hance spent the next four years courting the 501(c)(4) and 501(c)(3) leadership. Hance entered the 1990 primary with polls showing him with 38 percent of the vote; Williams entered the race with 4 percent of the vote. On primary election day, Williams won with 61 percent of the vote to Hance's 15 percent.

What happened? There were different reasons, but I will deal with how Williams acquired 87 percent of the pro-life/pro-family vote, which was 32 percent of the total Republican primary vote.

Most of the 501(c)(3) and 501(c)(4) leaders personally endorsed Kent Hance, but because their organizations by law could not use their data or assets for campaign activism, they could not legally promote Hance through their most valuable mouthpiece—their mailouts.

On the other hand, COPAC did its name gathering and research as a PAC. Therefore, we could release our research showing Hance's past pro-choice voting record, and we could mail this information to 2,600 leading activists and pastors and to 132,000 households that were identified as pro-life/pro-family.

After a specific purpose direct-mail piece was released, we could then call these people and urge them to join Clayton Williams' team. I could answer questions as the leader of COPAC, not losing identity or having to be careful not to be partisan because we were a political action committee. I organized sixteen hundred volunteers in two hundred counties and raised over seventy-six thousand dollars for the PAC.

# CHANGING PUBLIC OPINION: THE SENATORIAL BRIEFING FLOW CHART ORGANIZATION

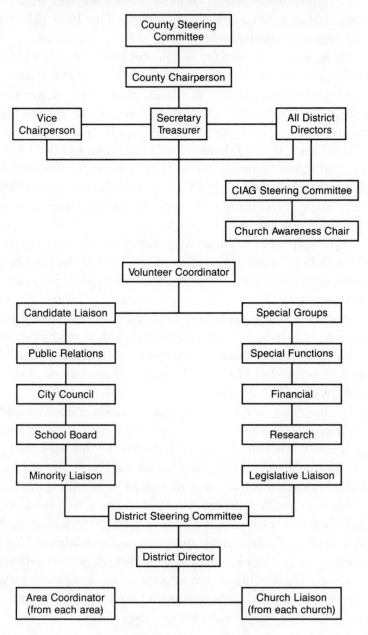

The fight was fair because those leaders who wanted to work for Kent Hance could not do so as leaders of their organizations, nor could they use the assets of their organizations.

You cannot fight a political war with your troops and assets locked up inside the barracks. You must have your database and assets available to your PAC and the candidate of your choice.

## The Moses' Plan

Just as Moses organized the tribes of Israel, your PAC must organize and mobilize Christian voters. Small groups of like-minded Christians should be formed or identified in every neighborhood.

An area coordinator should be responsible for ten to twelve precinct coordinators. The precinct coordinators should supervise ten to twelve neighborhood captains.

Neighborhood captains should be given a list of all known Judeo-Christian traditional-values households in their neighborhoods. That should give them a nucleus of people with which to form prayer and action groups. Every Christian traditional-values voter should be identified and assigned to a neighborhood captain.

**Ways to identify pro-family traditional-values voters:**
- Obtain evangelical church membership lists.
- Obtain membership lists of pro-family legislation or issues groups.
- Have a petition drive on pro-family legislation or issues.
- Use voter registration drives to register Christian voters, and copy the information before you turn it in.

Each commissioner's district has approximately twenty thousand homes; each city council or state representative district has about fifteen thousand homes. This may vary from state to state.

**Sample way to divide a commissioner's district or county:**
- Obtain a county district and precinct map from the county clerk or election office.
- Divide the district into ten areas.

# THE PAC CHAIN OF COMMAND

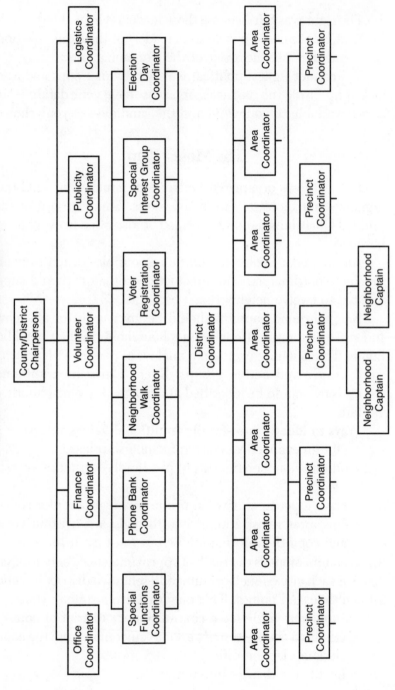

- Divide each area into ten precincts.
- Divide each precinct into ten neighborhoods.
- Assign fifteen traditional-values voter households to each neighborhood captain.

Using this plan, every Christian traditional-values voter should be assigned to a neighborhood captain, who can then organize small groups or solicit the support of existing neighborhood Christian groups. Each district would oversee over 20,625 homes times ten districts for a total of 206,250 homes. Yet, no neighborhood captain would be responsible for more than fifteen households. Thus, in one three-hour period, all leadership could be contacted. The use of automated telemarketing machines would greatly increase the efficiency of gathering names and determining what volunteers will do.

**Ways to network:**

- Compile and categorize church lists: evangelical, pentecostal, charismatic, and activist.
- Do voter registration drives and copy the new registration information.
- Do mailings, with a survey insert to determine voter interest in issues such as taxes, education, and abortion.
- Use petition drives based on such issues as strong abortion laws and tough pornography laws to gather names.
- Volunteer for campaigns or be involved in campaigns to gather names and workers.

A name that you know nothing about is almost useless; therefore, call the names on the list or mail a survey to learn as much about the people on your list as possible.

**Who you should network:**

- Eighty-five to 90 percent of all people going to charismatic and pentecostal churches will vote according to Judeo-Christian traditional values.
- Pro-lifers may be moderate on issues other than abortion due to the fact that so many are Catholic and Democrat. In our survey, we found that pro-lifers are usually 75 percent to 85 percent true Judeo-Christian conservatives. These

percentages are based on polls conducted by the American Education and Resource Foundation in 1988.

- The listeners of Christian radio should hold Judeo-Christian traditional values, and 10 percent to 20 percent of them should become actively involved.

**Goal setting:** If people do not choose measurable goals, they will have no way of determining whether they have been successful. Goals also inspire accountability. If we share our goals with others, we will be more likely to fulfill them, and others can hold us accountable. Goal-setting is also a key ingredient to positive group dynamics.

At the end of every public program have some form of goal-setting. If there is an outside speaker, ask the speaker what he or she would like the group to do. Have some kind of response sheet and ask the people to share what they feel God would have them do regarding the matter at hand. A secretary should write down what tasks people volunteer to do. Check at the next meeting to learn what has been accomplished.

Small groups encourage people to share ideas, so during your meeting try to take twenty minutes in small groups to discuss objectives. Have the groups summarize their suggestions.

**Long-range planning for your local organization:** Most groups make the mistake of trying to build or fund an organization from the top down and centralize data, finances, and resource information. However, every level of an organization needs to retain access to resources in order to be an effective force in their voting area.

## A Plan for Organizing

**First, organize the smallest unit as if it were the most important.** The precinct chairperson should be given a budget, voter lists, and equipment to operate his or her precinct. All equipment, names, and other property belong to the county organization.

The area coordinator's primary responsibility should be to build strong precinct organizations. Where does the money come from to recruit leaders, do precinct newsletters, and pay for computers? One way is to convince people to invest in the political action committee in their neighborhood, precinct, and state, with a portion of their donations going to national programs.

Your organization must have a clear set of bylaws, goals, and plan of action. You should have a job description for each assigned task, and you should thoroughly train all workers. If someone performs unsatisfactorily after being informed of his or her inadequacy, remove that person from the position and put in another. Christians need not be timid about expecting the best from each other.

The area director should take responsibility for visiting pastors or church members and trying to form issue awareness groups in every evangelical church in the district.

*The Neighborhood Captain*

The neighborhood captain is responsible for establishing a neighborhood group that can be a prayer group, a political awareness group, or a combination of the two. Each neighborhood chairperson should be supplied with a list of all known conservatives and Judeo-Christian traditional-values voters in their neighborhood.

Neighborhood captain duties can vary. The neighborhood captain could:

- call on every family identified by headquarters.
- organize a neighborhood prayer group.
- organize a neighborhood awareness group, such as a crime stopper group or a block party.
- visit new people moving into the neighborhood and give them voter registration cards.
- take on specialized duties during a campaign.

*The Precinct Coordinator*

The precinct coordinator may or may not be a party precinct chairperson. The precinct coordinator is elected by the members

of the precinct committee, which is comprised of the neighborhood captains and the Judeo-Christian voters of the precinct:
A precinct coordinator's duties include:
- attending area meetings.
- recruiting neighborhood captains.
- sending names of new people to data centers.
- coordinating the PAC's activities in that precinct.
- meeting with neighborhood groups and encouraging them in their programs.
- calling on the churches in the precinct and setting up church issues awareness groups.
- being the coordinator for a campaign's activities in that precinct.

## Planning the PAC's Introductory Precinct Meeting

The precinct coordinators should meet together to plan initial public precinct meetings. Determine at that time the most popular program to draw people to the first precinct meetings. Organize the program to draw as many Christians as possible.

Make a list of all born-again Christian couples and singles living in each precinct. Invite each one personally to an initial precinct meeting. To do this, divide the names among the neighborhood captains and other interested participants. Make sure that each potential voter is invited by the one who knows him or her best. After people have been personally invited, send out reminder postcards.

Meet with all those who were invited to the initial meeting but did not attend. Go through the response sheet with each of them to determine their areas of interest and possible participation in your PAC.

The introductory meeting:
- Have light refreshments available.
- Have nametags on hand for everyone.

- Welcome everyone to the meeting.
- Explain that the purpose of the meeting is to organize Christians in the neighborhood and to determine how they can have an impact on their community and nation.
- Introduce the neighborhood captains and others who are sponsoring the meeting.
- Introduce the speaker or topic of discussion. A possible topic for a speaker could be "The Importance of Christian Involvement in the Political Process" or another issue of interest to the group.
- Ask several people to pray for the concerns voiced by the speaker.
- Explain the legislative issues for the evening, ideally using a prepared outline of a letter. Ask each person to write a letter, framing the response in his or her own language. (For married couples, one spouse could use the home address and the other a work address.)
- Collect the letters and stagger their mailing over the next week.
- Suggest that people contribute toward postage costs.
- Solicit volunteers for your PAC.

## Aiding Christians in Their Political Giving

Christians need to be instructed in the importance of giving to political causes. Money wins elections, and Christians need to understand their responsibility in this area.

The leaders of the conservative movement in your area should meet and determine the twelve organizations and candidates recommended for support for the following twelve months. Each month gather material about the organization or candidate selected. Duplicate a cover letter and combine it with pieces of literature describing the organization or candidate. Be sure to include the name, address, and telephone number of the organization or candidate. Also indicate whether or not contributions are tax deductible.

*First Precinct PAC Meeting: Objectives*

This meeting is run by the area coordinator or district director.

- To get people to come to the first meeting, pass out fliers in churches, distribute posters or fliers at Christian schools, place ads on Christian radio, and work telephone banks.
- Select precinct coordinators (and remember Paul's direction to Timothy in choosing leaders).
- Review the objectives, go through the job description of the church issues awareness coordinator, the precinct coordinator, and the neighborhood captain.
- Have a map showing the designated voting area this group is responsible for.
- Make a list of the names and phone numbers of everyone who joins the committee.

## Area Coordinators

The area steering committee is made up of precinct coordinators and church issues awareness captains (one from each church involved).

An area meeting could be held monthly or bimonthly. The officers should be area coordinators, vice-coordinators, and secretary-treasurers.

The area coordinator could be appointed or just emerge naturally from a group, but once an organization exists its bylaws should specify a time to elect a permanent area coordinator. The members of the committee could choose the coordinator from among themselves.

## Area or District Planning Meeting

**Preparation:**
- The precinct coordinators in designated areas should meet to plan the year's meetings, arranging for outside speakers and electing an area chairperson.

- Write all the information for the month's lobbying letter on a blackboard or poster.
- Provide light refreshments.
- Provide name tags until everyone gets to know each other.

**The program:**

- Welcome.
- Pass out the agenda.
- Give two minutes to each precinct coordinator to give an overview of each precinct.

## The Area General Meeting

Can Christians change public opinion and government policy? To answer this question one must analyze how people form opinions and agendas.

People learn values through emotional conditioning. They are influenced by role models. If you can host emotionally positive meetings with Christian role models, you should be successful in organizing like-minded people.

Michael J. Weiss's *The Clustering of America* gives a vivid portrait of the nation's forty neighborhood types, their values, lifestyles, and eccentricities. Weiss's study proves that careful analysis can almost predict what type of cereal is in the cabinet and what magazines are subscribed to in a given neighborhood. The forty types of neighborhoods, from "blue blood estates to public assistance," can be determined by analyzing buying trends, reading habits, voting patterns, and other data. By planning our meetings and neighborhood divisions so as not to mix cluster types, we can have an influence on the voting trend of an area.

One should study the Prizm method developed in 1974 by Jonathan Robbins. Robbins, who founded Claritas (Latin for "clarity"), devised a wildly popular target-marketing system by matching zip codes with census data and consumer surveys. He named his creation PRIZM (Potential Rating Index for Zip Markets) and programmed computers to sort the nation's 36,000 zip codes into forty "lifestyle" clusters. We can use that kind of system for planning an organizational growth pattern along demographic lines. It will also explain why we will be successful in some precincts or voting areas and not in others.

When the Reagan administration attacked Social Security as a drain on the budget in 1981, the Democratic National Committee (DNC) used the neighborhood cluster for a direct-mail appeal to rarely tapped, moderate-income Democrats for support to reinstate the proposed cuts. After sending its appeal to the subscription list of *Prevention* magazine, whose readership included many over-fifty-five Americans, the DNC discovered that the pitch worked best in clusters whose poor residents rely on Social Security as a subsistence income, where issues affecting the elderly hit close to home, and where residents sympathized with the plight of older Americans. Thus, pressure was put on Reagan by the very clusters that put him in office. The programs were reinstated. You can use the cluster system in your own area for building victories.

## The Plan

Utilizing the methodology from the book *The Clustering of America*, we can

- build our geographic boundaries around clustering model types.
- invite speakers that influence cluster types. Whereas Pat Robertson might influence one cluster type, Colonel Oliver North or Chuck Colson would influence other cluster types, even though all are Christian.

A well-planned and broad-based organization will not try to put different cluster types in the same room and expect it to be homogenous. Keep like clusters with like clusters. Plan your district meeting not to be confrontational but acceptable to the clusters in that district. You may have to make adjustments in order for your organizational boundaries to be homogenous.

To build a successful Christian organization, one must build it on the successful common denominator of Jesus, not just on issues and especially not on doctrine.

The meeting program should be planned three months in advance.

An area meeting should be held at least six times a year where all the precinct organizations can gather. The district organization should have at least three meetings per year for all area organizations.

Area meetings should be held in a library or a public building, not in a church. If you must use churches, it is good to vary the church building used.

## Meeting Agenda

Welcome everyone to the meeting and introduce the speaker. Ideally a speaker should not speak for more than half an hour. If appropriate, allow time for questions.

**Recruit church coordinators.** Assign each church and organization in the area to committee members. Have each committee member become the coordinator in his or her own church and be responsible to recruit a coordinator from other churches. Make sure that every church and organization on the list has been assigned a committee member. Once a coordinator has been recruited, place his or her name in the "Church Coordinator" column. Make sure all coordinators are committed Christians.

**Gather names of Christians.** One of your goals is to collect the names of Christians from every church and organization on the list.

- Ask your friends and acquaintances for additional names.
- In rural areas, often one person will know all the committed Christians in a county or town. Give him a copy of the telephone directory and have him mark the names of all committed Christians. You will be able to obtain addresses and phone numbers from the directory.

**Sample call script.** If you do not have a personal contact in a church, call the pastor for assistance. You might use the following conversation as a guide.

"Hello, my name is _____. I've been meeting with Christians from various churches in our area to see what we can do to influence local and national government. Would you be able to give me the names of people in your church who might be interested in meeting with us?"

When the pastor suggests church members, ask for their phone numbers as well. Invite these people to your next meeting.

## The Area Coordinator

The area coordinator should review the list of evangelical Christian churches and organizations in the voting area and give this list to the church issues awareness committee chairperson.

The area coordinator should also delegate the responsibility of name gathering. If no one on the area committee has any contacts at a particular organization or church, the committee member responsible for that organization should call one of the organization's leaders (in the case of a church, its pastor).

Endeavor eventually to have a representative from each Christian organization and evangelical church in your voting area on your area steering committee.

**Be sure to gather names only from organizations and churches with Judeo-Christian traditional-values memberships.** If there are conservative members who are not born-again, ask a member to share with you just the names of the born-again members.

## Area Steering Committee

The area steering committee is made up of the precinct coordinators from each precinct and the church issues awareness group coordinators from each church.

### *Duties of the Area Coordinator*

The area coordinator is a member of the district committee, which meets quarterly. The area coordinator helps recruit volunteers, the precinct chairperson, and the neighborhood captains.

The area coordinator is responsible for picking up material from the district coordinator, distributing it to precinct coordinators, and functioning as a precinct coordinator in any precinct that doesn't have a precinct coordinator.

The area coordinator, during a campaign, is responsible for the phone banks in their area. The area coordinator is responsible for communicating with the party precinct chairperson and for recruiting people to run for party precinct chairperson. The area coordinator is in that position to build a successful area network, and the area will only be as strong as its leader.

The area coordinator could be the precinct chairperson in his or her own precinct, if the workload is manageable. The responsibilities include

- reviewing methods and sources for gathering names.
- reviewing the recruiting of church committee captains.
- reviewing the job description for a church committee captain.
- recruiting a church committee captain for all churches and organizations assigned. You may initially want to approach someone about becoming a contact person within an organization or church. Share some of the possibilities for what a church coordinator can accomplish through his or her own church.
- recruiting and training people to run for party precinct chairperson and be precinct coordinator for your group.
- working with the churches and pastors when a precinct doesn't have a precinct chairperson.
- holding quarterly meetings featuring speakers.
- presiding over the area meeting.
- aiding other appropriate campaigns and lobbying.
- planning area meetings.

☆  **93**  ☆

- administrating any special projects in the area.
- helping precinct coordinators with their meetings.
- communicating with precinct coordinators about issues, legislation, candidates, and local problems.

# The District Board

The district board is made up of all the area coordinators from each area and the church issues awareness group (CIAG) coordinator elected by all the CIAG coordinators from the area. Dual organizations, such as the church issue awareness group might be operating under 501(c)(4) rules and therefore must be careful not to do a project in a church that would put its 501(c)(3) status in jeopardy. It's best for the church issues awareness group to be part of an organization that just uses the church as a meeting place and is not an official church group.

## *Functions of the District Director*

The district director is elected by the district board. The district director's functions include
- presiding over the district steering committee.
- attending precinct meetings or area meetings.
- visiting pastors and holding pastors' district meetings.
- recruiting and training people for area and precinct positions.
- visiting officials on the district school board, county commission, or city council.
- choosing chairpersons of the following committees: education, city council, county government, special programs (for each program), legislative, congressional, candidate liaisons, research, publicity, finance, minority liaisons, and county board or state senatorial district.

The county board or state senatorial district may have the same organizational structure. If the senatorial district is located in an urban county, then it can become the division for the county structure. If the county is smaller, use the county commissioner lines or state representative lines to divide the district.

The chairperson of each committee makes up the county board corresponding committee.

The county chairperson could be selected at an annual meeting to serve no more than one two-year term. That will help keep the organization fresh.

All district chairpersons, area chairpersons, and church awareness officers vote for county board officers. The officers should be chairperson, vice-chairperson, and secretary-treasurer. The entire board votes on what committees should be standing committees.

### Functions of the County Chairperson

The functions of the county chairperson are to preside over the county steering committee, recruit a district director, hold county pastors' briefings, meet with candidates, function as a liaison to other organizations, and hold training classes for coordinators.

The county chairperson is a public relations liaison with the community and should appoint a representative to attend most political or community-related activities. The county chairperson will chair the county board and be the general administrator of your local PAC. The county chairperson should have a monthly or bimonthly breakfast with activist pastors. The county chairperson could be a member of a regional steering committee and needs to meet with other coalitions and organizations on a regular basis.

The county chairperson must remember to have a checklist and timetable with a master assignment sheet. Your PAC must also be a team effort. The county chairperson must get committee chairpersons and coordinators in place as soon as possible and be sure they know their jobs and how to carry them out. They must also be open to new ideas and better ways to do things. Remember Proverbs 6 and be careful that suggestions from county chairpersons don't become destructive criticism fostering strife.

The county chairperson should work with all pastors and special group leaders. Remember that pastors have been called by God to tend their garden first, so be willing and open to work with their designated representative.

Don't forget to build an alliance with all appropriate groups but do not lose sight of your purpose: to elect Judeo-Christian traditional-values candidates to office and to insure passage of traditional-values pro-family legislation.

There are many activities your PAC can do besides those related to political campaigns. By attracting people to the organization that have other interests besides specific candidates, the activity base of your organization can be broadened. The following is an example of what other goals COPAC was able to accomplish.

## Broadening the PAC's Activities

An organization built with a broad base, positioning itself between government, the private sector, and the church can work on many needed projects. Such a base will give your members a chance to lead people into salvation and help with related problems. An example of where Christian influence needs to be exercised may be within your local community action agency. Nationally, such agencies oversee millions of dollars in private sector and government grants; they oversee and fund projects such as meals-on-wheels for the elderly, education programs for the illiterate, help for people in financial crisis, shelters for the homeless, shelters for battered women, and funds for job training.

Elections to community action agency boards are federally regulated and held every two years in communities across the nation. Community action agencies have been around since 1963, but few state representatives, city council members, and party leaders, know about the election process or the power of such agencies. Since being elected to the board of the community action agency in Bexar County, Texas, we have brought the evangelical community face to face with problems of the poor and elderly. I have made use of hands-on programs using federal, state, and private funds. Dr. David Kitely, pastor of Shilo Christian Fellowship, Oakland, California, has used funds and provisions of this kind of agency and others, such as a $150,000-grant to aid the people living near his intercity church, which has stretched his church budget and meets the needs of thousands. In the past liberals have been experts in this kind of activity. No wonder the poor and people on fixed incomes turn to them at election time.

Your organization can become the leader in your community, helping to solve social problems from a biblical perspective, through the community action agency and other government and private sector grants.

The county chairperson, coordinator, and your PAC should be sensitive to minorities in your community. In the past, most voters of the minority community were diehard Democrats, but there has been growth in the minority evangelical church indicating a possible shift in voting trends. Liberal social workers, agencies, and liberal candidates neglect biblical pro-family issues and legislation, leaving the evangelical minority poor without an advocate. Unless Christian political groups recognize this, no one will fill the gap. The Christian community must put priority on running for boards and filling positions in social service. We must work with churches to find godly solutions to social as well as moral problems.

Jesus and the apostles spoke much on living a faith that met all the needs of the people. They did not concentrate solely on morality. For every area the modern church has neglected, the government has taken over. We must reverse that trend. We have the same duties Jesus gave the apostles and disciples to carry out.

To win the heart of the people—black, white, brown, yellow—we must have a socially aware and moral political agenda. We may not have the funds to solve social problems, so we must serve as Joseph, Obadiah, and others did within government, meeting our brothers' and sisters' needs.

## Committees within a 501(c)(4) PAC

The committee on education would monitor the school board and the curriculum of the school and help to fight illiteracy.

The committee on city government would monitor council meetings. It could assign a member to each council person in order to establish lines of communication. Someone should become familiar with the city charter and general regulations.

The committee on taxes might be divided into county, city, and school tax subcommittees and would be responsible for monitoring minority budgets and proposals and preparing reports.

The committee on legislation could be divided into state and federal subcommittees. Someone should establish communication with office holders through trips to the state capital and possibly to Washington.

The committee on public policy would be a think tank to produce papers and research supporting the work of the other committees.

The committee on political parties should teach PAC members about how to be active in the party, the party structure, and the function and rules of a political party.

The committee on candidate liaison would monitor new candidates and decide which candidate to back. The members assigned to evaluate each incumbent should give a report. This committee should meet with each candidate under consideration for support.

The special group coordinator committee is made up of a member from each Christian special interest group in the community, such as pro-life and home school groups. The special group committee should also, through the group's leadership, establish a person in each organization to recruit campaign workers and form a get-out-the-vote committee.

The special group coordinator should locate all groups (neighborhood organizations, tax reform groups, gun clubs, and so forth) that may support certain legislation together.

# Mobilizing the Christian PAC

**The committee on media** should publish your newsletter or monthly bulletin to keep your members informed. This committee should also prepare press releases and develop communication with the media. The committee may also want to do a local cable show. Your local cable company will give you one hour, production equipment, and teach you how to produce the program. Once produced, you can distribute the program to other cable companies in your county if you are in an urban county. We have found that sometimes other stations will air the program on Sunday or late at night for a small fee.

Many organizations have started a radio program on their local Christian station. Such radio programs are good places to run public service announcements on getting out the vote or features on the candidates and issues. You may find the station in your area very cooperative.

The media committee chairperson needs a team of people responsible for working with the PAC and the candidates it supports to coordinate news releases. No news release should be done on a candidate without notifying the candidate first, unless your committee is a nonconnected committee. Remember, a candidate's staff may be afraid of the religious right and might attempt to control your PAC. Don't let that happen.

**The publicity committee** is responsible for media endorsements of candidates, for news releases on the PAC, and for informing the public of important issues. Effective publicity can and will be a major asset to the success of your organization.

The publicity committee should prepare for talk shows and should coordinate letter-writing campaigns. The committee helps supply the director and candidate with information about local issues and concerns.

The committee should also prepare sample letters to the editor, with an endorsement enclosed. Phone numbers of PAC representatives and local officials could be included. Remember that advertising should be a recruiting tool. Every ad should have a number for a potential volunteer to call.

Being a conservative Judeo-Christian PAC, you may be dealing with a hostile media, so be very accurate. Don't rant and rave, but don't be afraid of confrontation or controversy.

**The committee on prayer** must remember that the evangelism of one person could change a nation. Jesus began with teaching the apostles. We will change this nation and bring it back to Christ when we bring our neighborhoods back to Christ.

We must pray daily for God's conviction and guidance. Prayer warriors and "watchmen on the wall" are imperative for successful Christian grassroots involvement.

We must keep the light of integrity on all areas of authority, holding each leader accountable to the whole. We must "walk in the light as He is in the light." Don't shy away from using biblical principles of leadership in your organization. Remember His grace.

**The committee on finance** is an important committee for planning fund-raising projects. There might be three separate bank accounts and multiple funding sources. Books and records should be kept on each division.

Church-related projects dealing with education, social, or issues awareness programs can be paid for with tax-exempt 501(c)(3) funds. You may find large contributors may want a tax deduction. The 501(c)(3) has this advantage. The church may also help fund the church issues awareness group when it is formed as a 501(c)(4). The givers to those programs should be kept separate and reminded that gifts are tax deductible.

## Assessing Dues

You might distribute dues so each level of the PAC can have the funds to function. That also keeps from centralizing control in the county board. You may also find that your PAC can get special discounts at stores and should consider applying for a commercial vender license because of its size. Your members may then find their dues not to be a burden. A rural county, of course, would have fewer members, but would also have a smaller budget.

For example, a typical urban county or a state representative district contains 120,000 households with perhaps 10 percent being evangelical. If 10 percent join you, you have 12,000 times $18 per month in dues or $216,000 per district. So it is up to all of us in a grassroots network to get as many families involved as possible.

I recommend dues of eighteen dollars per month per family membership. For their membership dues PAC members get the right to vote and hold office in the organization, the right to solicit funds and get help if they are candidates, and a city or state benefit package with such benefits as consumer discounts, discounts at restaurants, and group insurance. There may be retailers who will provide such savings to your organization to encourage members to patronize their business. Such benefits can allow members to pay dues without adding a financial burden.

Let's break the eighteen dollar per month dues down into each PAC division level and see the potential for funding.

- Precinct budget. Fifty families or individuals in a precinct paying eighteen dollars per month, of which five dollars is for precinct use, could support a precinct budget of $250 per month.
- Area budget. Ten precincts at an average of fifty memberships per precinct could support an area budget of $1,500 per month, with three dollars of dues going to the area budget.
- District budget. This amount can be collected from four areas with 600 people per area. With three dollars of dues taken from each membership, a six-thousand-dollar per month district budget can be supported.
- County budget. With seven districts per county and two dollars assessed from dues, fourteen thousand memberships would support a county budget of twenty-eight thousand dollars per month.
- State budget. With two dollars assessed memberships in each congressional district, a $140,000 per month state budget could be supported.

The last three would give you a substantial amount to put in your PAC fund or send to a national organization. It could be as much as $210,000 per year.

### Financing Local Power

Keeping the majority of your money at the county level is important. If we do that while supporting appropriate national organizations, we will all do better. Your organization may not reach the size of dues-raising model described above, but by using the same methodology, you will be able to change your area and guarantee a godly inheritance for your children and grandchildren.

We can learn from organizations such as the John Birch Society. Educational programs alone will not guarantee moral leadership. We must work to elect that moral leadership with education, prayer, and participation in the political process.

### Finance—Types of Contributions

A 501(c)(4) organization can receive gifts from churches, corporations, and individuals. The funds are nonprofit, but the gifts are not tax deductible. They can be used for voter registration, public awareness programs, candidate forums, and nonpartisan get-out-the-vote (GOTV) drives.

A 501(c)(5) fund is PAC money that is nonprofit, but not tax deductible. Individuals may contribute, but money from churches and corporations cannot be accepted. Such funds can be used for all the above mentioned projects and also used to directly affect an election.

**The campaign committee** should have a phone bank, walk program, sign production, and volunteer recruiting subcommittees. The function of these committees, especially during a campaign, is discussed in full in later chapters.

## An Example of Coalition Building

In 1988 the state PAC, Texans for Justice, which raised over $250,000, organized a coalition of several PAC's and other organizations in Texas. Its job was to elect conservatives to the Texas Supreme Court. It endorsed six candidates, five Republicans and one Democrat.

This coalition of COPAC, Texas Grass Roots, homeschoolers, and people who had supported the Robertson presidential campaign organized over three thousand volunteers statewide. The coalition had phone banks in 180 counties, shipped thirty thousand yard signs, and distributed 4.5 million pieces of literature. I was privileged to head the networking and planning for this project. We made use of every organization's existing lists of volunteers and leaders. We had eleven automated telemarketing machines, five computers, and a phone bank of ten people calling statewide. The use of resources was maximized by satellite down links.

Richie Martin, who was a state director for Americans for Robertson, produced an hour special on the candidates, emphasizing the differences among the candidates and clarifying the moral issues. By using satellite technology that cost less then twenty-five hundred dollars, the special was broadcast to locations statewide where leadership and volunteers were gathered. The next day three thousand video copies of the program were made, and within days 535 boxes containing yard signs, voter report cards, candidates' brochures, address lists of supporters, videos, and instructions on what to do for the next fourteen days were shipped to leaders throughout the state.

Five of the six endorsed candidates won statewide Republican seats, which had never been done before in Texas. One candidate won by only twenty thousand votes—that's three votes per precinct.

Once you have begun to build your organization successfully on a broad base and sound godly principles, it will become a formidable factor in the community. But remember: power may corrupt. Keep your books open (that's why its good to be a PAC; your books are public records), rotate your leadership, and remember the constitution our forebears made. We are a republic, not a democracy.

# CHURCH ISSUES AWARENESS GROUPS

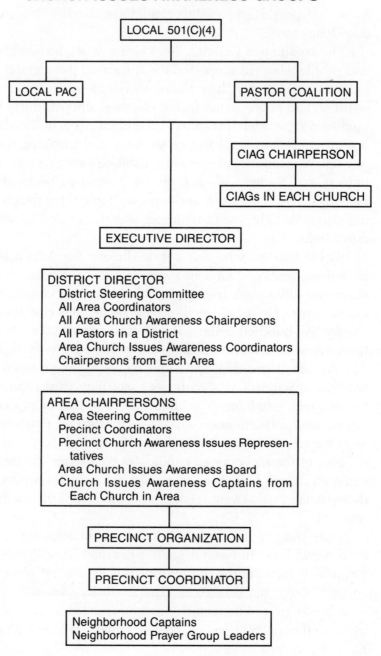

LOCAL 501(C)(4)

LOCAL PAC

PASTOR COALITION

CIAG CHAIRPERSON

CIAGs IN EACH CHURCH

EXECUTIVE DIRECTOR

DISTRICT DIRECTOR
District Steering Committee
All Area Coordinators
All Area Church Awareness Chairpersons
All Pastors in a District
Area Church Issues Awareness Coordinators
Chairpersons from Each Area

AREA CHAIRPERSONS
Area Steering Committee
Precinct Coordinators
Precinct Church Awareness Issues Represen-
tatives
Area Church Issues Awareness Board
Church Issues Awareness Captains from
Each Church in Area

PRECINCT ORGANIZATION

PRECINCT COORDINATOR

Neighborhood Captains
Neighborhood Prayer Group Leaders

# PASTOR COALITION
# ON TRADITIONAL VALUES

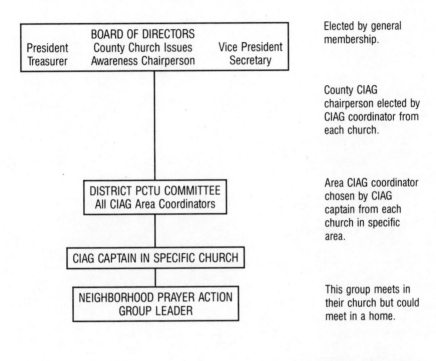

Membership committee comprises all pastors in the county.

Elected by general membership.

County CIAG chairperson elected by CIAG coordinator from each church.

Area CIAG coordinator chosen by CIAG captain from each church in specific area.

This group meets in their church but could meet in a home.

Each member of the CIAG in a specific church chould have an NPA group.

The CIAG group or a similar group functioning in a church is an asset-gathering entity. Your group should supply names to your PAC and encourage members to volunteer for campaign or lobbying activity. Remember, a 501(c)(3) or a 501(c)(4) cannot show partisanship. Your church organization or asset-gathering organization should be a 501(c)(4). The 501(c)(4) can form its own political action committee.

The Christian PAC should not force doctrinal beliefs on anyone. Let us instead work to elect moral people to office who believe in Judeo-Christian values and support a constitutional government.

# The Pastors' Coalition

The pastors' coalition associated with a PAC can meet by district or county. The coalition has six primary objectives.

1. To provide a forum for pastors to express their needs, desires, and social concerns.

2. To create and express a pastors' perspective on the spiritual status of the community, state, and nation.

3. To gather information on candidates and issues from reliable sources.

4. To become aware of the political process, pending legislation, and the performance of incumbents.

5. To learn how to involve church members in the political process.

6. To learn what state or federal laws govern their activities.

The coalition should be a group of local pastors or pastors' representatives. Meeting days most favorable to pastors are Tuesdays or Thursdays. Breakfast meetings should be no more than ninety minutes long, starting normally at 7:00 A.M.

The coalition members may serve while they are involved in active ministry and should have a priority to serve in harmony and unity of purpose. Proposed new coalition members will be recommended and voted on by the existing membership. All coalition members will vote on officers who serve at the pleasure of the coalition membership. Nomination for officers will be submitted yearly to the nomination committee appointed by the coalition president. Other officers will be vice-president and secretary-treasurer.

## Purpose of the Coalition

The pastors' coalition is unique because its membership has a common profession. The coalition will consider its members as individuals in their involvement in coalition activities and in no way perceive its members as representing a church or its membership in any legal form. In addition, the coalition does not hold any church or its membership financially responsible for the coalition.

The coalition is organized for the sole purpose of defending the basic constitutional rights of churches and to work against legislation that has eroded or would erode Judeo-Christian traditional family values.

Official positions on issues will be approved by a majority vote of the coalition membership. An official position paper will then be authorized. After a position paper is written, it will be returned to the membership for ratification. Ratification requires a 90 percent vote of members in attendance.

Resolutions supporting proposed legislation will be made in a resolution committee and submitted to the membership for approval by a majority vote. Such resolutions would establish the coalition to be

- against abortion.
- against pornography.
- for biblically based principles and against secular humanism.
- against drug or substance abuse.
- against sodomy (homosexuality or lesbianism).
- against mandatory sex education.
- against governmental encroachment of parental rights.

- against child abuse.

Financing the coalition should be accomplished by private donations and fund-raising. The goals of the individual members of the coalition and the coalition as a corporate body should be to

- educate the public on traditional-values issues.
- clarify its position on issues by presenting position papers.
- call candidates and officeholders to accountability and publicize their positions on the issues.
- organize a voter registration committee to ensure that church members are registered to vote.
- cooperate with church issues awareness groups to organize nonpartisan get-out-the-vote efforts on election days.
- encourage the public to participate in partisan politics.
- encourage Christians to run for precinct chairperson and elected office.
- have nonpartisan educational sessions about the issues in their respective churches.

The following is a list of the officeholders for your coalition and their responsibilities:

The *rotating chairperson* will preside over monthly meetings using *Robert's Rules of Order*, serve as a spokesperson, and appoint members to nomination, public relations, and resolutions committees.

The *vice-president of finance* will be president at the meeting in the president's absence, coordinate fund-raising activities, and oversee the budget.

The *vice-president of candidate liaison* will develop a committee to monitor the city council, state representatives, state senators, and school board officials; maintain a file on incumbents, and work with the PAC in the distribution of candidate report cards.

The *vice-president of community relations* will educate other pastors about the coalition, communicate with other organizations, and organize praise rallies. A praise rally is a musical event where the church choir or Christian entertainers perform—no preaching.

The *vice-president of organization* will coordinate phone banks in each church for information distribution, organize voter registration drives in each church during the months of October and March, and form a committee to encourage minority participation.

The *vice-president of political action* will organize the get-out-the-vote (GOTV) drive for April, November, and other election times, and aid in organizing church issues awareness programs.

The *secretary-treasurer* will have the responsibility of filing state reports, developing the budget, chairing the budget committee, planning fund-raisers, taking minutes, and informing members of meeting times and venues.

The *executive director* or *executive secretary* (on a consultant basis) will implement the plans of the coalition, keep pastors informed concerning issues and events, conduct research on issues and candidates, monitor the legislature when in session, coordinate publicity and press conferences, interact with committees, and be answerable directly to the coalition's board of directors by giving a written and/or oral report.

## The Church as a Place of Education

How the church and its people are to participate in the political system is not taught effectively in our churches. We must become knowledgeable in running for office and knowing a position's qualifications. We must understand the responsibilities of the voter, and participate in the Republican or Democratic party system, from the precinct caucus to the national convention.

The church can offer classes on the Christian's civic responsibilities. It can be effective in the political process by
- asking those who want to serve in the political arena to contact a designated person in the church.
- setting up classes in PAC and/or party involvement.
- holding a mock precinct convention.

- encouraging members to become party precinct chairpersons.
- urging church members to identify other voters by address, phone, and precinct so precinct candidates can encourage them to attend the precinct caucus after the general election.

# The Do's and Don'ts of Political Activity

The following is excellent advice from Alan P. Dye and was published by the *Biblical News Service* of Costa Mesa, California.

Pastors are justly concerned about the legal effects of political activity on themselves and their churches. Churches are exempt from federal tax only as long as they do not participate in political campaigns. Federal election law also places restrictions upon political activity by individuals and institutions, particularly corporations. The scope of proper political activity varies from case to case, but the following do's and don'ts are applicable to many cases.

### *Political or Electoral Activities*

A pastor may individually and personally endorse candidates for political office.

A church may not endorse candidates for political office, and a pastor may not endorse candidates on behalf of his church.

A pastor's personal endorsement may be made from the pulpit if it is clear that it is his personal view and not that of the church.

A pastor may allow his name to be used as a supporter of a candidate in the candidate's own political advertisements. The pastor may be identified as pastor of a particular church.

Churches may engage in nonpartisan voter registration and voter education activities so long as such activities are not intended to benefit any political candidate or party.

# Grassroots Politics

A church may allow political candidates to speak on church premises in the same manner that civic groups and other organizations are allowed. If civic groups and other organizations are required to pay rent for using church property, the political candidate should be charged the same amount.

A candidate should not be allowed to appeal to a congregation at a church service for funds to be used in a political campaign.

Lists of members of the church congregation may be provided to candidates for use in seeking support or raising funds only if such lists are made available to other individuals and organizations. If a charge is normally made for such a list, the candidate should pay the same amount. No favoritism should be shown among candidates in providing a list of congregation members.

A church may not establish a political action committee.

Pastors and other like-minded individuals may establish a political action committee, but care should be taken that the committee is separate from the church.

## Legislative Activities

A church may not engage in "substantial" educational legislative activities. The substantiality of legislative activities is usually measured by reference to church expenditures. Expenditures of less than 5 percent of an organization's total budget are generally not considered substantial.

A church may give its mailing list to a legislative organization if such a list is made available to other organizations also. If a legislative organization is given more favorable terms, the cost of the mailing list would be considered a legislative expenditure.

A pastor may engage in lobbying activities as an individual without adversely affecting the tax exempt-status of his church.[1]

---

1. Used by permission of Alan P. Dye. For a copy of the full legal opinion, write *Biblical News Service*, P.O. Box 10428, Costa Mesa, CA 92627.

## Position Papers

A position paper is a statement of an organization's or a candidate's position on a specific issue. I believe these guidelines should be of assistance to a pastors' coalition.

- A position paper should contain only one issue.
- A position paper normally is one to two pages.
- A position paper should contain clearly and concisely defined concepts.
- A position paper should be readable and of interest to the general public.
- The facts presented should be specific, and your position should be reinforced by other authorities.

The following are examples of position papers based on a biblical perspective of social issues. They are taken from Plymouth Rock Foundation fact sheets.

## Governmental Responsibilities of Ministers

It is the reasoned conviction of the membership of the [your coalition's name] that the moral, cultural, and economic decline of America is directly related to the failure of Christian pastors to speak with a clear voice about the freedom-giving and life-protecting values of the Bible.

We therefore resolve to begin to preach and teach not only in the churches for which we are responsible but also in the community at large. We understand that to carry out that responsibility, it is necessary to take biblical stands not only in our pulpits but also in other public forums, including the councils of government. We must also teach our church members to speak out and act on their beliefs through the use of the ballot. We are further committed to instruct all in our community who will listen that responsible citizens can return America to moral and cultural sanity by supporting candidates that uphold Judeo-Christian values.

Nowhere in the Constitution of the United States of America can the modern doctrine of separation of church and state be found. Nor can that doctrine be found in the writings of the men involved in the formation and ratification of the Constitution. The principle that is stated, which has prevailed until the middle of this century, is the constitutional prohibition that restricts the federal government from establishing a religion or prohibiting the free exercise of religious beliefs. A nation that was morally asleep accepted the concept that the church could be "separated" from the state and suffer no decline in the quality of life. Without moral restraints, we now suffer an imprisonment of fear. The crucial concern in America should not be the separation of church and state but the separation of the state from the church.

Substantiated by Supreme Court decisions and historical research, the religious and moral foundations of our nation were based on Christian ethics. We, who present this paper, take our stand not only from historical and traditional assurances but also from the biblical knowledge that the church is "the pillar and ground of the truth" (1 Tim. 3:15).

As further evidence that we reject the current philosophy of separation of church and state, we submit that both the church and the civil government are created and ordained by God. Each has its proper sphere of authority and responsibility. Neither is to rule over the other. Each is to assist the other in its proper calling. The church has the ministry of teaching values and salvation to governments as well as to individuals. The politician, then, is not exempt from receiving proper instruction from the church. Should he or she fail to hear, then the error should be correctly and thoroughly proclaimed. It is the civil government's place to protect the rights of its citizens to free speech, assembly, and of protection from criminals. The government should render justice from knowledge of biblical morality and defend our shores from foreign invasion. It is not the place of civil government to invade our homes with immoral dogmas, license our churches, and deny a church's constitutional right to fulfill its ministries.

We believe that civil government is not the only government

ordained by God. The family is a government having authority in its God-ordained sphere. Church and business organizations are also properly ordained governments. Civil government does not have scriptural license to invade the integrity of other governmental entities that exist in society. Because we are living in an era of radical de-Christianization, we have seen civil government assume a role far beyond its scriptural authority. Other governmental structures are being emasculated and dehumanized by civil government which is abandoning historical Christian values and constitutional restraints. We are therefore committed to resist the error of philosophies that are foreign to our national foundations. We are compelled to teach and instruct our congregations and communities biblical values and proper government, whether that proper government be the government of the family, the church, the business, or the state.

## Secular Humanism vs. Judeo-Christian Values

We believe that from our work related and social experiences, the majority of the people in this community are not in agreement with, nor profess, the dogmas of secular humanism. We also believe that the majority of the people in this community are

(1) directly opposed to abortion on demand after the third month for any reason other than incest, rape, and when the life of the mother is in danger.

(2) directly opposed to sodomy (homosexuality) being protected or promoted as an alternative lifestyle and that those who engage in such practices should not be protected as a minority group.

(3) directly opposed to magazines, movies, or any form of entertainment that glamorizes obscenity or promotes pornography as an art form.

(4) opposed to any legislation or interpretation of legislation that would diminish their rights as parents, placing their children under state jurisdiction.

(5) opposed to state mandated sex education that usurps the

authority of the local school board and the prerogative of parents. Sex education that neglects the Judeo-Christian moral value of chastity and condones the free distribution of condoms through the school is not acceptable.

## Sodomy (Homosexuality and Lesbianism)

Sodomy (homosexuality and lesbianism) and perverse sexual acts such as incest and bestiality have been documented in history in societies and cultures before their disintegration. Romans 1:28 gives a clear account of God's position on unnatural and immoral sexual sin. In the Old Testament Leviticus 20:13 states, "If a man lies with a male as he lies with a woman, both of them have committed an abomination. They shall surely be put to death. Their blood shall be upon them."

For the past decade the gay rights movement has gained momentum throughout the United States. Over one hundred gay PACs in forty-five states have raised millions of dollars to openly support candidates for local, state, and federal offices.

We are opposed to gay rights antidiscrimination ordinances. We are opposed to the consideration of homosexuality or lesbianism as an alternative lifestyle. We are opposed to defining the family as anything but the union of a man and woman in marriage.

We hold that neither homosexuality nor lesbianism was created by God but is a psychological or physical condition that can be corrected. We believe that the Christian community must love the person but stand against the sin. When a person chooses to embrace a homosexual or lesbian lifestyle, we will urge others to shun him or her. We will encourage the community to oppose any legislation legalizing sodomy and to oppose any officeholder or candidate that accepts any form of sodomy as an alternative lifestyle.

## Obscenity (Pornography)

The pornography industry is an eight-billion-dollar-a-year industry that is polluting the minds of many Americans.

Material depicting sexual degradation, domination, and humiliation, as stated in the 1986 Pornography Commission Report is currently a major segment of the pornography market. Using sophisticated technology to set up communication networks throughout the United States, the child pornography industry has grown enormously in the last fifteen years.

We believe research proves that the widespread distribution of pornography is linked directly to child abuse, rape, and sexual crime. God's Word is clear about ridding the land of degradation and perversion.

We encourage the enforcement of our present obscenity laws and ask for the strengthening of those laws so as to discourage the open display of any pornographic magazines that anyone under the age of eighteen may see. We advocate the change of federal communication laws that allow obscene material to be viewed on television or by satellite transmission. We encourage the acceptance and implementation of the recommendations of the Attorney General's report on pornography.

We encourage the public to boycott all stores selling pornographic material, call or write local television stations to ban obscene material and the depiction of sexual acts outside of marriage, call or write newspapers asking management not to carry advertisements for X-rated movies or stores dealing with pornography.

## Abortion

Abortion is the number-one killer in the United States.[2] From 1973 to 1987 an estimated twenty million babies have been aborted.

---

2. Statistics on abortion are from the Plymouth Rock Foundation, Marlborough, N.H.

Fallacy: Abortion will reduce dependence on welfare. *Fact: Welfare has tripled in the same period with millions of dollars going to tax-funded abortions.*

Fallacy: Most abortions are performed in the first three months and not after the fetus is viable. *Fact: An estimated 50 percent of all abortions are after viability, with many babies left to die outside the womb.*

Fallacy: Abortion is a solution to unwanted pregnancy and has no medical or psychological side effects to the mother. *Fact: Research and statistics prove mothers can have physical and psychological problems affecting their future health.*

Fallacy: Abortion is an alternative to having unadoptable babies. *Fact: The backlog of families waiting to adopt children would adequately deplete the supply of babies that are now aborted, and the majority of the families would be able and willing to pay medical costs. Adoption would save lives and over 800 million tax dollars per year.*

We believe abortion is murder as stated by God's word. "You shall not murder" (Exod. 20:13). "If men fight, and hurt a woman with child, so that she gives birth prematurely . . . but if any lasting harm follows [eg., the child dies] then you shall give life for life" (Exod. 21:22–23).

We therefore propose to enact legislation stipulating

- that no abortion can be performed after life begins, except when the life of the mother is endangered.
- that the same rule and policies applied by the medical profession to life maintained by a life support system be applied to a fetus.
- that the facts on abortion as currently performed be made public, that such information be provided through public media and through the school system to show the reality of abortion, and
- that public funding be provided equally to all groups educating and counseling women about abortion whether pro-choice or pro-life, or no such funding should be allowed at all.

We oppose the use of any taxes or federal monies for abortions. Are not government officials to be servants ("ministers") of God (Rom 13:1–4)? Since we are a "government of the people," how then can we as citizen magistrates serve God by decreeing that abortion is "legal" when it breaks God's law? We will encourage the public to oppose any legislation promoting abortion. We will work to defeat any candidate who supports abortion.

## Acquired Immunity Deficiency Syndrome

Acquired Immunity Deficiency Syndrome was first called Gay Related Immune Deficiency because it was first found only in the homosexual community. AIDS now has become an epidemic that has spread to heterosexuals. AIDS is a fatal disease that slowly destroys the body's immune system, leaving a person vulnerable to a host of infectious diseases, including forms of cancer. The AIDS virus has been found in saliva, tears, mother's milk, urine, perspiration, and blood. It is believed to be transmittable only by direct exposure to large doses of virus in blood or semen.

An estimated five million people in the United States now have been exposed to the AIDS virus, and between 10 and 30 percent will die from AIDS. AIDS is now the fourth leading cause of premature death in New York City.

Therefore, we believe that every effort should be made to help the person with AIDS medically and financially and to protect society. We recommend

(1) that AIDS be classified as a communicable disease and all policies regarding contagious diseases be implemented;

(2) that antibody testing should be required of anyone in the food handling profession who is in direct contact with the public;

(3) that persons carrying the AIDS virus be prevented by law from having any further sexual contact without full disclosure of the diagnosis to all partners; and

(4) that establishments proven to permit illicit sexual behav-

ior on the premises should make certain such behavior does not occur. Any establishment not complying should be closed.

We do not agree that the promotion of condoms is the proper preventative for this disease or even a major deterrent. We believe chastity, abstinence, and monogamy are effective deterrents. We also demand a full disclosure of all government research done on AIDS.

We do not intend to promote mass hysteria or alienate any person that has AIDS, but it is the purpose of the government to protect all of its citizens from a devastating plague.

## Drugs and Substance Abuse

Some form of substance abuse has plagued society for centuries, but this should not be a reason to allow such abuse to continue. Society must now show that any type of abuse of drugs is unacceptable.

Drug abuse is not only costing millions of dollars but also is robbing our societies of the capabilities of our youth and adults who are abusing drugs.

We feel that the only deterrent to substance abuse is to increase criminal fines and prison terms and swiftly dispose of legal cases, initiate testing in all portions of the community, and adhere to rigid drug-free standards in sports, the media, and politics. People in those professions should unite to police their industries.

We urge all pastors to educate parents and youth on substance abuse. Special recognition should be given in the media and school systems to those who complete educational programs.

We urge all businesses catering primarily to youth to promote a drug-free environment.

## Legislated Mandatory Sex Education

We oppose legislation that states that explicit sexual material will be taught in a designated sex education class. We believe that a biblically founded traditional-values approach should be used in sex education. We fully support and urge the teaching of premarital abstinence.

We believe sex education of any explicit form should be taught in the home and that parents have the right to ask that their children be exempt from any teaching of sex education in school.

We believe that the Bible clearly provides guidelines "to train up a child" and to avoid the "dangers of sexual sin." We do not believe it is a public educator's role to indoctrinate a child in his or her interpretation of acceptable sexual practices or behavior.

The sex education provided in schools should be limited to a study of biological functions and anatomy. Such instruction should not be in a coed class and certainly not be given prior to puberty.

We believe progressive approaches to sex education are in clear violation of parental authority and do not adhere to biblical standards. We believe that research and documentation prove that legislation advocating explicit sex education has failed to produce positive results.

Therefore, we maintain that promotion of safe sex and contraception before marriage is morally wrong and that abortion as an alternative to pregnancy is morally wrong. We also insist that explicit explanations of sexual intercourse be prohibited in coed classes, and that sexual intercourse before marriage and in any form other than a husband and wife be recognized as morally wrong. In every way possible we will urge the people of this community to oppose any legislation, school board candidate, or public officeholder favoring mandatory sex education.

## Church Issues Awareness Group

The church issues awareness group (CIAG) should encourage members from each church to be a part of PAC efforts or to work in campaigns. The CIAG is a perfect group from which to recruit neighborhood PAC captains, since the church's members are usually located in various sections of the community.

*The CIAG coordinator* recruits people to run for precinct chairperson, organizes voter registration drives, establishes twelve-week issues awareness seminars, and recruits people to work on campaigns.

*The district church issues awareness group chairperson* is responsible for organizing pastors' coalitions. The chairperson could also have a district or county legislative symposium for the pastors.

The *pastors' coalitions* will conduct research and produce position papers on current issues, organize a trip to the state capital to meet with legislators and visit committees, and organize a luncheon or breakfast for pastors and their representatives.

## Dinners for Pastors and Legislators

Organizing dinners for pastors and their legislators is a worthwhile activity and such dinners can serve to
- introduce the pastors and legislators to each other.
- present the current issues and legislation that will be of interest to the Christian community.

To ensure the most successful dinner possible
- invite pastors from the state representative's district.
- have up to nine pastors and one state representative at each table.
- have a prior reception for state representatives, pastors, and business people from that district.
- designate a head table for three state senators and four parachurch leaders.

*A sample budget:*

| | |
|---|---:|
| Packets—150 | 150.00 |
| Dinner—200 pastors × $8 | 1,600.00 |
| Ten reception rooms—200 | 300.00 |
| Decorations | 300.00 |

# The Pastors' Coalition

Price for Business Leaders

| | |
|---|---|
| 11×3=33 pay $100.00 | 3,300.00 |
| Two corporate sponsors | 2,000.00 |
| | 5,300.00 |

## *The First Church Issues Awareness Group Meeting*

The first district or area CIAG meeting is initiated and organized by a person appointed by the pastor or the district director.

To publicize the meeting distribute fliers in churches and place announcements in church bulletins. Ask pastors to announce the meeting and mention it at area or district meetings.

## *How to Organize Church Issues Awareness Groups*

To begin the process of organizing church issues awareness groups, make a list of the Bible-believing churches in your voting area. Write the names of those churches and other conservative organizations in the first column entitled Church/Organization in the format given below. The remaining columns will be filled in during future steps.

| Church/ Organization | Recruiter | Church Coordinator | Names Obtained |
|---|---|---|---|
| | | | |
| | | | |

Next, assign each of the listed churches and organizations to PAC committee members. Have each committee member become the coordinator in his or her own church plus be responsible for recruiting other coordinators. Make sure that every church and organization on the list has been assigned to a committee member. Be sure that every church has a CIAG coordinator. Make sure all coordinators are committed Christians.

The most important job for the CIAG coordinator is to gather as many names and addresses as possible of committed

Christian voters. To collect names you should make a list of all the Christians in each church or organization and ask PAC precinct coordinators to indicate who are committed Christian members.

If you do not have a personal contact in a church, call the pastor for assistance. You could have a conversation similar to this:

"Hello, my name is _____. I've been meeting with Christians from various churches in our area to see what we can do to influence local and national government. Would you be able to give me the names of people in your church who might be interested in meeting with us?"

When he suggests church members, ask for their phone numbers. Call everyone on the list and invite them to your next meeting. If they do not come to the meeting but are still interested, meet with them personally.

## Helpful Hints for Beginning a CIAG

• *Obtain permission from your pastor.* Make an appointment to meet with your pastor. Share with him why you feel it is vitally important to form a CIAG in your church. Present the issues facing the Christian community in a concise and understandable fashion. If it is available, show him the CIAG video we have produced. Pursue his support, but don't expect him to take an active role.

• *Schedule a time and place.* Check with the pastor and schedule a specific time and place to hold the first CIAG meeting. The church is a good meeting place because of its location and familiarity.

• *Place announcements in your church bulletin.* Talk with the church secretary and ask him or her to put announcements in several of the Sunday bulletins prior to the actual date of the meeting.

• *Pass out flyers that explain the CIAG and announce the first meeting.* Flyers should be made available after services and should provide information about the CIAG as well as the time and place of the meeting. It is helpful to print the flyers in bold type on colored paper.

## Helpful Hints for Organizing the First CIAG Meeting

• *Show a video (if available) that explains the purpose and goals of the CIAG.* You can make a simple video yourself or order one from Charles Phillips, P.O. Box 701267, San Antonio, Texas 78270. The video is an excellent tool for beginning your first meeting because it will answer a lot of questions. It will also give the people an idea of what to expect as they become involved in their CIAG.

• *Describe the CIAG.* The purpose of the CIAG is to train Christians and inform them of their role in civil government. The CIAG will periodically distribute information on issues and candidates, set up voter registration drives at election times, and set up telephone trees or phone bank systems to relay information concerning upcoming votes before Congress, the state legislature, and the local city council.

• *Give the job description of the CIAG coordinator and the agenda for the CIAG.* The CIAG coordinator will recruit members, call meetings, and delegate activities. The coordinator will also be the contact person for the CIAG. The agenda will be different in each church, but basically the members will need to attend the scheduled meetings, be an active part of a committee, and be committed to helping the CIAG reach its goals.

• *Elect a person to be the leader and develop a list of committees.* A leader/coordinator needs to be elected for the CIAG, after which a list of members should be developed. Ask persons at the meeting to write their names and home/work telephone numbers.

| NAME | HOME PHONE | WORK PHONE |
|---|---|---|
| _____ | _____ | _____ |
| _____ | _____ | _____ |
| _____ | _____ | _____ |

Committees to focus on specific groups and issues—for example, committees to oversee local city council affairs, the state legislature, and the U.S. legislature—should be developed at this time. Other committees would focus on such issues as abortion and pornography. Some sample committees include school board, city council, commissioner district, state legislature, candidate liaison, pornography, voter registration, issue education, phone bank, and abortion.

• *Begin first project.* Now the CIAG is ready to begin its first project. This project should be a petition drawn up on a hot issue, such as pornography, abortion,or homosexuality. This will help identify like-minded people in your church and is an excellent tool to send your legislator. The first project may be one of a variety of things, depending on the current issues at the time your CIAG becomes active. An example would be to obtain signatures to petition the state legislature to oppose legalization of sodomy in Texas (an important issue at present). Another idea would be to make addresses of the local congressmen and state representatives available to the church so that members could begin to inform them of their views on abortion, pornography, home schooling, and any other current issue affecting the church. As the CIAG becomes informed through Christian organizations and publications, newspapers, and magazines, you will see that ideas for projects are endless.

## Church Issues Awareness Group Class

The CIAG in each church could organize issues awareness classes over a twelve-week period. The teacher on each issue could be a layperson or a PAC committee member.

# The Pastors' Coalition

The following is a sample letter by Rev. Terry Gayle at University Baptist Church in San Antonio, Texas, recommending the successful church issue awareness class to other churches. The pilot program was devised by Mrs. Billy Zimmerman of his church and a member of COPAC.

*Dear Pastor,*

*Recently, during our regular church training hour, our church put together a special series entitled "Issues and Answers." The issues were the major moral issues that we face today. Those in attendance were very responsive, and we discovered a number of well-known and qualified speakers who were eager to work with us.*

*Enclosed is a listing of the issues and the names of those who spoke on each subject. We were fortunate to have a very qualified layperson who organized the complete program.*

*Our people responded with a great deal of interest and enthusiasm. Each speaker presented a video and then spoke on a particular issue. Time was given for questions. Our young people sat in on the video portion and then left for their own discussions.*

*I found that each speaker was very cooperative and eager to be of assistance to our church. They presented views that were generally in harmony with my own. All in all, I was very pleased with our guest speakers and recommend them to you.*

*May the Lord bless your ministry and give guidance to your leadership.*

> *Gratefully,*
> *Rev. Terry Gale*
> *University Baptist Church*

## Examples of CIAG Classes

The following classes were given at University Baptist Church, San Antonio, Texas, by Mrs. Billy Zimmerman and may serve as examples of the type of CIAG classes you might organize. Each class consisted of a fifty-five-minute presentation.

SUBJECT: Secular Humanism.

VIDEO TITLE: *Let Their Eyes Be Opened.*

VIDEO DESCRIPTION: Secular humanism is shown to be in direct conflict with Christianity as presented by a clergyman and a humanist. Issues discussed include abortion, situation ethics, pornography, public education, and sex education.

SPEAKER PRESENTATION OUTLINE: The speaker describes the activities of Concerned Women for America, its national and local organizations, and its founder, Beverly LeHaye. The speaker leads a discussion of the effects of secular humanism locally.

SUBJECT: Drug Abuse and Drug Rehabilitation.

VIDEO TITLE: *Medical Aspects of Mind-Altering Drugs.*

VIDEO DESCRIPTION: Detailed information is given on various types of drugs, the symptoms of abuse, and the destructive physical, social, and spiritual results of drug abuse.

SPEAKERS: The speaker reinforces the video presentation, leads discussion, and describes local efforts to rehabilitate drug abusers. To get speakers contact local law enforcement or local programs such as Teen Challenge.

SUBJECT: Abortion.

VIDEO TITLE: *A Matter of Choice.*

VIDEO DESCRIPTION: Provides a hard-hitting approach to abortion by dispelling common worldly myths. Includes a clinical view of abortion in progress with scenes of aborted babies and the testimony of mothers.

SPEAKER: The speaker uses visual aids to provide statistics on the cost, number, and social consequences of abortions since 1972. For speakers contact your local Christian crisis pregnancy center or Right to Life chapter.

SUBJECT: Legislative Issues: Christians as Civil Authorities.

SPEAKER: The speaker gives an overview of the legislative system at the state level, especially the power of governor and lieutenant governor, the legislative committees and subcommittees, and the ideological composition of present state legislature. The speaker also explains the scriptural basis for Christians in positions of civil authority. For speakers contact local Christian politicians or Christian PAC representatives.

## Sample Issues for Topics

| | |
|---|---|
| Abortion | Lobbying |
| Child Abuse | Political Activism |
| City Council | Pornography |
| Domestic Violence | Satanic Worship/Cults |
| Drugs | Secular Humanism |
| Education | Sex Education/Teen Promiscuity |
| Homosexuality/AIDS | Teen Problems |
| Legislation | |

## Resources for Material and Speakers

American Family Association
Biblical News Service
(214-850-0527)
Christian Action Council
(202-544-1720)
Christian Coalition
Christian Doctor
Christian Legal Association
(703-941-3192)
Citizens for Decency
(602-995-2600)
Citizens for Excellence in
Education
Concerned Women of America
(202-628-3014)
Crisis Pregnancy Center
Department of Drug
Enforcement
Eagle Forum (202-544-0353)
Educational Research Analysts
(214-753-5993)

Elected Officials
Family Research Council
(202-393-2100)
Federal Bureau of Investigation
Focus on the Family
(714-620-8500)
Gun Owners of America
(703-321-8585)
Intercessors for America
(703-471-0913)
Local Law Enforcement
Morality in Medicine
(212-870-3222)
National Council on Child Abuse
and Family Violence
(818-914-2814)
National Right to Life
(202-626-8800)
Plymouth Rock Foundation
(603-876-4685)

☆ **129** ☆

# The Campaign Strategy

In order for your PAC to successfully affect a candidate's campaign, you should have a clear strategy based on information gathered from polls, surveys, and voting trend research.

The campaign operations of a PAC must have clear, distinct directions for leaders and volunteers.

An operations manual for the campaign should be assembled and distributed to key workers. The manual should contain a summarization on candidates, operations data, the voting history of the target area, your organization's position on issues, and whom to contact for additional support.

Carefully and prayerfully choose the candidates your organization will support. Know the personal history of each person your organization intends to support and who else is giving support. You may not want to choose a candidate just on the basis of whether he or she can win. You may want to determine if the candidate is running as an Elijah, using a political platform as an expanded pulpit, or as an Esther, winning with a broad based coalition and serving as an officeholder who does not compromise God's precepts and standards.

PAC members should recognize that a political campaign can

be used to make your positions on issues clear to the community or party, force the other side to utilize resources against you, give the PAC practice in a campaign, mobilize Christian voters to help other candidates, expose the candidates to the community-at-large and to the Judeo-Christian community, defeat deceptive leaders.

Many political races seem impossible to win in the beginning but have been success stories in the final analysis.

## Prince or Prophet

There are some distinctly unusual characteristics regarding Christian candidates as opposed to regular party candidates. The typical party candidate usually has a broad platform that appeals to a variety of special-interest groups. Pro-family, pro-life, and Judeo-Christian issues are combined with tax, gun control, and defense-spending issues. The candidate's campaign staff will probably put the candidate in the middle of the road with regard to controversial issues in order to appeal to everyone.

The Christian PAC must be extremely careful not to allow professional campaigners to cause a candidate or supporters to compromise biblical beliefs.

Senator Bill Armstrong (R—Colo.) is an excellent, effective politician who has not compromised his Christian principles. He is known in Washington as a man who lives by them.

Senator Jesse Helms (R—N.C.) is a public figure with a role different from Senator Armstrong. He has been a lightning rod and a brazen standard-bearer of moral and conservative values. Both Armstrong and Helms have been effective, one as a "prince" and one as a "prophet."

### The Prophet

Over the past eight years, the typical prophet type of candidate has been a voice for the precepts and standards of the Lord God. It is not easy to be elected as this type of candidate, but it is not impossible. Examples of the prophet-politician include Senator Helms, former Congressman Siljander, Congressman Gingrich, and Congressman Phil Crane.

Many times prophet candidates are dependent on the provision of the Lord (see 1 Kings 17:6, 9). During the 1986 lieutenant governor's race in Texas, I witnessed God's anointed people providing support for David Davidson's prophetic campaign. Three Christian donors carried 80 percent of the financial burden. Davidson finished second in the primary and needed support in a runoff election. The people who had supported him in the primary could not provide support in the runoff, but God sent a Christian businessman who financed the major portion of the runoff campaign.

The prophet candidate frequently brings a word of rebuke and raises a moral standard to the people in power (see 1 Kings 18:17). During the eighties, many Christians ran for public offices against regular party candidates. Their presence and actions brought rebuke to those in power and moral direction to the people. Such prophets brought an uncompromising message to the voters, calling them to stand on His Word and not compromise the statutes and precepts of God.

The prophet candidate will make an Obadiah-type campaign worker nervous (see 1 Kings 18:9). Such a person may also serve in the party or in the government and is God-fearing and God-serving through the vision that God has placed in them. Normally they are the opposite of the Elijah-type and respond with anxiety to the actions of a prophet candidate or leader.

Obadiah-types are more pragmatic and will work with the existing order to bring change over a long period. History has shown that Elijah-types will make the Obadiahs' consistent and faithful work more effective. A principle to remember is that such change comes through confrontation, not from compromise. Legislators will begin to vote righteously, even if their personal habits are unrighteous, when they recognize the increasing strength of Christians at the ballot box.

Prophet candidates commonly have people serving them who will carry on and expand the calling (see 1 Kings 19:19). The group who follows the prophet candidate must recognize the calling and see the long-range vision. Over the past ten years most prophet candidates have disappeared from the political scene and have been replaced by someone who served them during the campaign.

In Oregon, for example, Joe Lutz ran in the 1986 Republican primary against a powerful liberal incumbent, Senator Robert Packwood, and lost by only 1.5 percent. One would think this was the beginning of a promising political career, but Joe Lutz is no longer involved in politics. One of his supporters, however, now leads the Oregon Alliance, a conservative group that formed for the campaign.

Pat Robertson may never return to active politics as a candidate, but his presidential campaign created new leaders and organizations in thirty states. Many who worked in his campaign have received positions with the Republican party on local levels. There will be those who plot against the prophet candidate, declaring the candidate's campaign method useless (see 1 Kings 19:2).

False leaders will predict victory against godly candidates. There are those who will plot against the prophet candidate. Yet, the godly candidate has a true understanding of the goals God has in mind. You will probably find that those who are plotting against the prophet candidate have a hidden agenda, especially antagonists from the Christian community. The opposition can always find a Christian humanist or a moderate to counter the statements of the prophet candidate. Frequently, the opposition and the media will try to create a credibility problem.

In the excellent book *Changing of the Guard*, George Grant describes the new leadership that has emerged in the last couple of years. Grant rightly recognizes that the leadership of the nineties must change the government by electing people who support Judeo-Christian values, fight for appropriate legislation, as well as hire bureaucrats and appoint judges who share the Christian ideology. We must have leaders who do more than write self-serving books. We must have leaders who are accountable for the millions of campaign dollars donated by the public. Our political leaders should spend those millions to build grassroots organizations, not to build self-centered kingdoms of media hype or amass personal wealth.

Evangelical Christian organizations and PACs that have been the political vanguard of the religious right have taken in over three hundred million dollars in recent years. What do we have to show for it? How have the contributions been spent? What have been the priorities?

We, the Christian community, must build local organizations, not simply send the money to national organizations. We must have local control and a local agenda which addresses concerns down to the county and precinct levels. In addition, we must concentrate on electing local candidates as mayors, justices of the peace, school board members, and to other local offices.

As members in Christian PACs it is our duty to demand recognition and results from officeholders, for we have given our labors, our funds, and our votes. As conscientious Christians, we have a great challenge before us. However, through perseverance and obedience to godly principles, we shall see results.

## The Esther or Prince Candidate

From the story of Esther we can build a description of a type of candidate who has a heart for God and His statutes and precepts. Esther's character traits will give us an understanding of certain principles that must be followed in a campaign. The Esther or prince candidate is usually a person who pays attention to detail, follows instructions, works with Christians and non-Christians within the system, follows standard campaign procedures, appeals to many factions, and obeys God's counsel (see Esther 2:6).

The prince candidate must continually keep his eyes and heart fixed on God.

Esther, we should remember, was directed by her uncle to follow the guidance of those in the king's court in order to be selected by the king. There may have been an understanding that by serving in the king's court she would be serving Jehovah, and thereby be a blessing to her people.

Many times it is those close to the prince candidate who have the vision, as Esther's uncle did. The prince candidate is obedient to such godly counsel (see Esther 2:7).

The prince candidate is frequently someone who is used by God to solve a specific problem. In the United States today some of the Christian heritage we hold dear and would like to practice has been ruled unconstitutional, such as praying in school and preventing the murder of the unborn. Christians need to support candidates who pledge to return our nation to its God-inspired destiny.

At times the counsel God has provided the prince candidate may not always be given by believers, but such counselors have the knowledge of what it takes to have a successful campaign. Christian counselors who have a heart for God's ways should be recruited (see Esther 2:8, 9). The candidate must be open with his or her counselors and be willing to accept correction and direction.

The hand of God on the prince candidate will be manifest through the provision of the assets to create a successful campaign. Thus, the candidate must have the financial resources and leadership qualifications. To gain the voter's confidence and establish credibility the candidate will require the proper credentials for the office for which he or she is running. Local offices may not require a college degree, but a higher office might. If a candidate has proven abilities in a lower office, such experience may be the best qualification.

Academic qualifications and perceived credibility are not as necessary for the prophet candidate as for the prince. The prophet candidate will be called by God to exhort believers and will be raised up by godly people. Both types of candidates can be acceptable to pastors and the pro-family, pro-life community.

In order to determine whether a candidate has potential, the party or financial contributor should check out the following:

candidate, steering committee, financial committee, endorsements, campaign organization, financial commitments, budget, research on voting trend, candidate vita, candidate's previous offices, campaign plan, campaign time live, media plan, research on opposition, and polls and survey.

This is the procedure for a targeted race: get strong people on the steering committee, get commitment on funds and assets, talk to the movers and shakers in the business community and local party, and meet with the party candidate selection committee.

## The Successful Campaign

The successful Christian PAC-supported campaign will require adequate financial resources. There should be a realistic, detailed budget showing the cost of each phase of the campaign.

An exploratory committee should estimate the financial and human resources needed for primary, runoff, and general elections. Supporters must be people willing to give time and money to each phase of the campaign. Thirty-five percent of your PAC's budget should be committed to specific purposes before entering a primary or general election. An individual or some friends may be willing to finance beginning efforts, if some of the money can be returned. Such loans, however, cannot exceed allowable contribution limits. The contributors must also be willing to understand that if there are no funds available for repayment, their loan will be considered a donation.

A candidate's personal funds or in-kind contributions should be listed as a loan. That will allow the contribution to be repaid to the candidate if excess funds are collected.

When tracking expenditures, make a spreadsheet starting with the amount of funds you have. Then subtract expenditures from that amount when orders are placed, not when the checks are written. That method will help you keep from ending the campaign with a large debt. Remember, it is hard to keep a clear head during a busy campaign, so set up systems to protect yourself. Keeping clear, verifiable campaign expenditure and income records is essential. The PAC must be willing to be accountable to its own people as well as to those it opposes.

The PAC should also research the number of votes cast in past elections in order to project a favored candidate's constituency. That can be done by analyzing the voting trend by party or by studying a candidate who has a similar ideology.

You should determine the number of Judeo-Christian households in the voting area, specifically identifying the pro-life, pro-family, evangelical, independent, Baptist, Pentecostal, and charismatic voters. If the PAC determines that there are two thousand registered voters, don't count on more than 60 percent to actually vote.

The candidate will need to be in contact with his or her constituency in order to solidify their support. The PAC should not assume that because the candidate says "I am a Christian" or "I am conservative," all Christians and conservatives will pledge their votes.

## Polls and Polling

If a candidate does not have the funds to hire a professional pollster, the candidate or PAC may obtain relevant information from a university, party, or nonprofit organization that has done polling. Remember, nonprofit polling is available to all candidates at the same cost, so find out what polls your opponent has used.

There are also several types of polls that a PAC itself can conduct.

A baseline poll will determine what a candidate's potential vote count may be. It is conducted by calling registered voters and assessing their support for specific positions on issues or their knowledge of your candidate. Such a poll determines how many of those voters called will vote for your candidate.

An opinion poll will determine what issues are important to

the voters and will allow a candidate to frame a platform to respond to those issues.

A name identification poll will determine how many people know your candidate by name. You may also determine any negative impact your candidate has by recording unfavorable responses.

A tracking poll will allow the PAC to track how well your candidate is doing as voters' perceptions of the campaign change. Such polls will vary according to the press coverage the candidate receives.

I do not recommend wasting money on hiring high-cost polling firms when they are not needed. Local races—such as school board, mayor, and county commissioner—will need some name identification and opinion polls; state and national level campaigns will need sophisticated polling. Usually volunteers can perform adequate polling, even if the results may not be as accurate as those of professionals. Be sure to get a good sampling of the voters—about three hundred is usual locally and nine hundred statewide. Don't poll your own supporters, and don't ask loaded or judgmental questions.

## Securing Assets that Grow

The candidate must have support from the leadership and opinion makers to ensure a viable campaign. The candidate not only needs endorsements, he needs proven leaders to serve as the leaders of committees for the campaign.

The following structure is suggested:

- A core group of six to ten people who can give credibility to the campaign and to help secure the assets needed.
- A top six-person team who can devote twenty or more hours a week to the campaign to fill the leadership roles.
- A support team of committee leaders who can devote ten to twenty hours per week to direct the committees and reach a predetermined goal.

- Adequate, dedicated volunteers to make up the committee groups to perform the tasks needed to win.

*Campaign materials.* A sufficient supply of campaign materials is needed by the candidate. While a sufficient supply of campaign materials doesn't need to be expensive, it does need to be:

- Excellent in quality, both in content and presentation.
- Clear and concise on the issues.
- An adequate presentation of the candidate's qualifications.
- Appealing to the voting group that the candidate is trying to persuade to vote and work for him.

*Necessity of God-given strategy.* A God-given strategy is a necessity for the candidate. "Now Esther had not revealed her family and her people, just as Mordecai had charged her, for Esther obeyed the command of Mordecai as when she was brought up by him" (Esther 2:20).

*Whether to identify as member of special interest group.* The prince candidate must decide if it is best to run as a representative of a certain special interest group or not. A person doesn't have to announce that he or she is Christian. Language and actions should prove that he or she is Christian.

Over the past decade, the media has given definition to role and type of person involved in various special interest groups. This should be a warning to proceed with caution. The media has portrayed the Christian candidate as a person who is single-issued, who will force doctrinal beliefs on people against their will, and who is fanatical about his or her beliefs. The Christian candidate would create a state church and force everyone to attend. Traditionally, the Christian candidate would be portrayed as illiterate, unenlightened, and irrational.

And so, as it was with Esther, it may be wiser not to totally reveal yourself until after elected.

*What type of campaign.* There are three different types of campaign, and the candidate will need to decide which is best for him or her.

- Event oriented. This type of campaign uses advertising

# The Campaign Strategy

and events in order to persuade voters to vote for the candidate.

- Issues oriented. This type of campaign uses issues to align the candidate with the majority of voters. The candidate stands for the issues of his supporters; this is usually a grassroots type of campaign.
- Personality oriented. This type of campaign uses the football star, war hero, astronaut, and so forth to run for office. The candidate's personality is highly acceptable by the voting public.

*Direct mail, phone bank, and block walking.* According to the finances available to the candidate, the candidate and advisors can determine the combination of direct mail, phone bank, and block walking to use for a winning campaign.

Typically, a local PAC-supported campaign can make use of some direct mailing of campaign literature, but will focus on phone campaigns and the candidate walking in neighborhoods to meet voters. The walking events should feature candidates in elections for school board, city or county council, or state house of representatives.

A statewide campaign or a campaign with a very large voting area would make extensive use of direct mailings, phone banks, and surrogate walkers. The walks would be manned by volunteers. Supporters would also hold coffee and video parties to reach as many voters as possible.

*Unregistered voters.* Many campaigns try to persuade the registered voter to vote for their candidate, while ignoring the many unregistered voters. It is particularly hard to unseat an incumbent without registering new voters. Therefore, a voter registration drive is a crucial part of your PAC planning, including a phone bank message on election day to get the voter to the poll.

*Advertising and material.* The PAC must determine what type of ads to run. Negative ads have taken much criticism in the last few years, but typically it is the media and the loser who scream "negative campaign." If an opponent has a voting record, or has made statements that illustrate an unfavorable position, then those facts must be made known to the voting public. I don't believe in insinuations or innuendoes, but if the negative information is verifiable, don't hesitate to use it if it gives real insight into the candidate's idealogy and philosophy. Remember, consultants try to hide the real candidate and create an image.

Positive media ads should give the positive attributes of the candidate and could feature the candidate's stands on key issues.

There are many types of campaigns a Christian PAC can be involved in, such as school board, city council, special boards, state legislature, and national congressional elections. It can be devastating to your organization's growth or existence if you stray from biblical values and support mere personalities. The pro-family PAC can build a campaign organization to aid several candidates, if it has spent time building an organization that stands for traditional values.

The Christian PAC must have a clearly defined plan and goals for supporting each candidate or favored legislation. It is important to have a well-defined operating procedure and a timetable for introducing the candidate to the Judeo-Christian community, a task requiring additional planning for a candidate who has poor name recognition.

Candidates with little name recognition will not usually have party backing during the primary and may depend heavily on your PAC for support. During the primary, it should not be assumed that the party rank and file is in agreement with the party leadership. Your PAC should also help identify independent and uncommitted voters and encourage them to vote for the candidate.

The registration of new voters is important, but these new voters should also be educated and informed about your candidate's platform. Their names, addresses, and phone numbers should be forwarded to the PAC election coordinator who will file them for future use.

*Publicity.* Using report cards, which highlight candidates' positions, is a good tactic, but may not be effective enough. Reproducing negative press clippings about an opponent and mailing them to the potential voters may be an effective way of communicating the true stand of an opposing candidate.

It is important to realize that the media may not be fair. Typically, it will show partiality to the incumbent or to the establishment's candidate. A Christian PAC cannot expect very much free media coverage (or what is called "earned media"), such as press conference coverage, publication of news releases (especially in large urban areas), or coverage by television. Rural papers or weeklies have a tendency to treat candidates equitably.

*Get-out-the-vote drives.* Do not assume that just because voters have been informed about candidates and issues that they will vote. Set up a solid committee in your PAC to coordinate the GOTV drive during the campaign. The GOTV committee should be a major activity during the last ten days of the campaign. The GOTV coordinator should at this time take on the administrative oversight of the entire campaign effort.

## Tips for an Effective Campaign

1. Phone banks identifying voters and securing volunteers should be functioning in every area of town. The PAC headquarter's phone banks should be monitoring all phone banks and recording their accomplishments. The night before election, phone banks should be used again to GOTV. Automated callers are an efficient use of time and can contact many voters and potential volunteers.

2. Poll workers should be at every polling place, not just at the favored locations. Even in a highly publicized election 5 percent of the people may come to the polls undecided. I have found for lesser known races the figure can go as high as 70 percent. In a 1990 primary for attorney general, on the day of the election we conducted a survey showing 68 percent of the people didn't know who was running.

3. The candidate's supporters should walk through their neighborhood at least sixty days prior to the election to do a sur-

vey. This is done to educate the voters and to estimate favorable votes. Walkers should walk again the weekend before the election or on election day. Car pooling to the poll and election day popcorn parties are a good way to get the neighbors out to vote.

4. The last direct mailing should arrive the day before the election. Never leave out any area of town. One vote for the opposition is two votes lost for your candidate. The PAC election coordinator should set vote goals for each precinct.

5. After the polls close, the PAC precinct captain or poll worker can watch the counting of the ballots, if he or she has a signed affidavit from the candidate to do so.

## The Campaign Management Structure

### District Director

The campaign district director (see organizational charts on pages 145 and 146) is in charge of the administration of the campaign in designated areas of a county or town. The district director may supervise as many as ten area coordinators and fifty precinct coordinators.

The district director is responsible for communications with all churches in the district and distributing campaign materials to area and precinct coordinators. The district director informs the area coordinators by phone of all directives.

The district director will help recruit area and precinct coordinators and make sure every precinct is manned.

The district director should meet with area coordinators to inform them of favorable legislation and to be informed of local needs. Participating pastors should attend such meetings as well as representatives of allied special-interest groups.

The district directors will help coordinate the function of each PAC committee, such as the phone bank and GOTV committees, in their areas.

The district director will need certain resources and do advance planning. If the district director doesn't establish deadlines, 90 percent of the workers will wait until the day before the election to start their jobs. The district director also needs the names, addresses, home and office phone numbers of his committee chairmen, precinct coordinators, captain manager, the press secretary, and other leaders in the official campaign organization.

The district director needs a map of the district showing precinct boundaries, which can be obtained from the city or county clerk's office or from the local election board.

## A PAC-SUPPORTED CAMPAIGN ORGANIZATION STRUCTURE

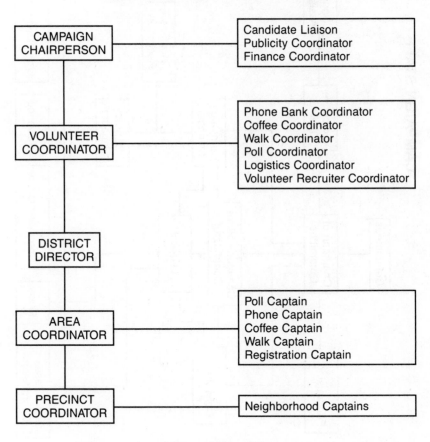

| CAMPAIGN CHAIRPERSON | Candidate Liaison<br>Publicity Coordinator<br>Finance Coordinator |

| VOLUNTEER COORDINATOR | Phone Bank Coordinator<br>Coffee Coordinator<br>Walk Coordinator<br>Poll Coordinator<br>Logistics Coordinator<br>Volunteer Recruiter Coordinator |

DISTRICT DIRECTOR

| AREA COORDINATOR | Poll Captain<br>Phone Captain<br>Coffee Captain<br>Walk Captain<br>Registration Captain |

| PRECINCT COORDINATOR | Neighborhood Captains |

# CAMPAIGN STAFF

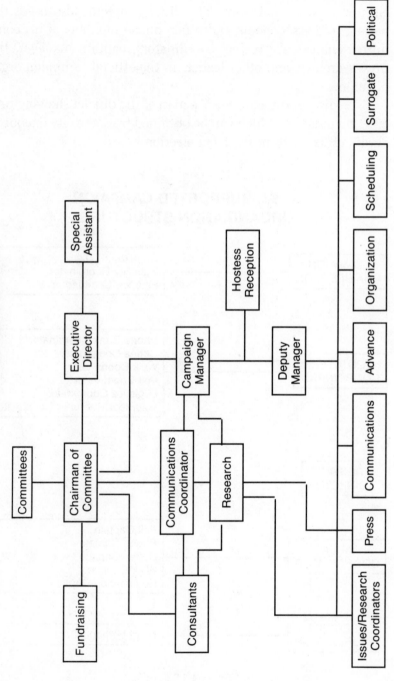

# The Campaign Strategy

The district director needs to know how many people voted in each precinct, where they voted, and for whom they voted.

The district director needs a copy of the election laws, which can usually be obtained from the secretary of state's office at the state capital, the city or county party headquarters, or from the local or state election board.

The district director must determine vote goals for all precinct chairpersons. The vote goal is the estimated number of votes that your PAC should realistically turn out from each precinct in order to win the election in the district.

A list of all registered voters in the district is vitally important to the district director and is generally available from the county clerk. In some states the list must be purchased. Sometimes, it can be obtained from party headquarters. A crucial list will be the one your PAC has compiled of the names of traditional-values voters. The district director will want to be assured of the delivery of this special group's votes.

The district director also should have the candidate's official campaign materials, plus statements by the candidate giving his or her positions on major issues, as well as biographical information and a record of public service.

## Area Coordinators

The area coordinators' duties during a campaign are
- to recruit precinct coordinators.
- to establish church issues awareness group coordinators and supply them with nonpartisan information on the candidates.
- to organize phone banks.
- to organize coffee or video parties.
- to pick up and distribute all campaign material for the area.
- to forward all information about volunteers and favorable voters to headquarters.
- to coordinate fund-raising events in the area.

☆ **147** ☆

## Precinct Coordinators

The precinct coordinators' duties during a campaign are
- to coordinate campaign activities in the precinct.
- to recruit precinct level volunteers.
- to work at the poll or recruit a poll worker.
- to recruit neighborhood captains.
- to coordinate the neighborhood walks in the precinct.
- to have coffee and video parties.

The precinct coordinator and the neighborhood captains should canvass the precinct to identify favorable voters. Each registered voter should be called on personally. Here is a sample approach:

"Hello, I am your neighbor, [name], and I am working for [PAC name]. Have you considered voting for [candidate] to represent us as [elected office]?

"I know this candidate and [his or her] beliefs, and I think [he or she] is an excellent candidate for the job. Can we count on your vote on [date]?"

Remember, your PAC effort should emphasize identifying, educating, and delivering the traditional-values conservative vote on election day. The role of the precinct coordinator is crucial in accomplishing these goals.

## A Check List for Precinct Coordinators

The following items are important for the precinct coordinator to have:
- a campaign calendar showing primary and general election dates and other important events
- the candidate's name and address
- the precinct vote goal
- the location of the polls
- voter registration requirements
- absentee voter requirements and voting locations
- sick and disabled voter requirements
- military voting requirements

- map of the precinct
- the names of registered voters in the precinct listed by their street address to be used for canvassing
- appropriate press releases, poll results, newspaper articles and other information about the candidate

The precinct coordinator's responsibilities during a campaign include picking up campaign material from the area coordinator and distributing it to neighborhood captains. The precinct coordinator will be responsible for placing signs at the polling places and distributing signs during the campaign. The precinct coordinator should be knowledgeable concerning the civic statutes of each neighborhood and is a vital link between the neighborhoods and the PAC steering committee.

The precinct coordinator should also be in contact with nursing homes in the precinct to ensure senior voters have a way to the polls or that they have voted by absentee ballot.

### Neighborhood Captains

The neighborhood captains are responsible for canvassing their neighborhoods to determine the number of favorable voters, in addition to passing out campaign literature and signs.

Neighborhood captains should also have block parties or backyard parties to get to know their neighbors. They should be encouraged to join neighborhood groups such as crime stoppers. The neighborhood captains are the key to success. They should help encourage neighbors to vote and may find hosting an election-day party a good way to do this.

### Volunteer Chairperson

The most important pre-election function of your PAC is the recruiting, training, and deployment of volunteers. The volunteer chairperson is responsible for the recruiting and job placement of volunteers. The volunteer chairperson should have a network of people in each conservative church and Christian organization distributing volunteer forms and returning them to the office to be processed. The volunteer chairperson's first objective is to work with the area coordinator and district directors to make certain each precinct has a coordinator. That coordinator could be a party precinct chairperson also. Each precinct should have a coordinator and at least ten neighborhood captains.

Upon receiving a completed volunteer form, the volunteer chairperson's team should contact the volunteer to verify his or her areas of interest. Next, the appropriate copies of the completed form should be placed in each of the coordinator's files.

All campaign letters to potential voters should have a volunteer application form and media advertisements should encourage people to volunteer. Phoning potential voters during the primary and general elections, as well as organizing block walks, should be a method to recruit volunteers. In addition, if each church in your community supplies fifteen volunteers, under normal circumstances you should have enough volunteers to conduct an effective campaign.

The volunteer chairperson should also recruit chairpersons for PAC committees and precinct coordinators for every precinct in the district, assigning them specific responsibilities and motivating them to fulfill their commitments.

Volunteer chairpersons should provide committee chairpersons and precinct coordinators with necessary campaign materials so they can do their jobs efficiently. They should keep all the volunteers aware of the campaign calendar.

The volunteer chairperson should replace nonfunctioning precinct coordinators with other volunteers who will work. This requires tact, discretion, and firmness.

The volunteer chairperson must see that each precinct coordinator is persuaded that achieving the precinct's vote goal will win the election.

The volunteer chairperson will try to make the PAC and candidate's staff function efficiently and harmoniously by promoting a team effort. A candidate's campaign staff, however, may not want your PAC assisting them. Your PAC must then decide to work independently.

**The candidate's liaison committee.** The candidate's liaison committee chairperson is the link between a candidate's campaign organization and your PAC. In consultation with the candidate's campaign chairperson and in harmony with the candidate's campaign strategy, the PAC and the candidate's liaison coordinator recruit and train the volunteers who serve as chairpersons of any collaborative campaign projects.

**The PAC's research committee** is a vital part of the campaign. Its function is to supply the PAC with in-depth information on the issues and the opponents.

The research committee should supply information for PAC position papers. A position paper should be brief with four or five suggestions for actions to be taken.

The PAC research committee should also examine

- the voting record of incumbents.
- ratings of candidates by conservative and liberal groups.
- relevant newspaper articles and speeches (usually there is a news clipping service at your state capital where you can get previous stories on incumbents).
- official candidate position papers or prepared releases.
- PAC questionnaires completed by the candidates.

In the performance of its duties, the research committee should

- make copies of all documentation.
- store documentation in a secure place.
- never manufacture or take out of context a candidate's statements.

**The finance committee** coordinator oversees the PAC finance committee. The PAC steering committee should make a budget for each primary and general election. All candidates desiring funds should meet with the steering committee to make their financial requests known. The finance committee for an election should not be confused with the finance committee of your PAC's general budget. Generally speaking, you will find PAC members and other Christians willing to give additional contributions during campaigns.

The majority of the budget or at least the amount necessary to do operations should be in place two months before a primary or general election. This would not necessarily be true for a publicity or special-events budget.

The finance committee is responsible for raising funds for your PAC and approved candidates. Neither the finance committee nor other PAC committees should borrow funds.

To meet the yearly administration budget, the PAC county board of directors should meet with the pastors' coalition and make a plan to raise funds and obtain pledges from individuals. Every PAC and campaign must have a general fund-raising chairperson who will coordinate efforts to raise sufficient funds to finance a winning campaign.

Here are some suggestions for fund-raisers:

*Personal solicitations.* Call on potential contributors and tell them the needs of your PAC. Describe one or two of the PAC's positions that might appeal to the potential contributor (such as taxes reform), ask for a specific amount, and try to collect a check immediately. If you plan to ask for a large contribution from an important person, telephone ahead of time for an appointment. The most important factor in successful fund-raising is to be enthusiastic about your goals. Remember, you are collecting money for your PAC, and it may be used for several candidates.

*Telephone solicitation* is an effective way to raise a lot of money. A combination of direct mail solicitation and telemarketing has been proven to increase contributions.

*Special projects* such as testimonial dinners, luncheons or brunches, receptions, bake sales, rummage sales, potluck dinners, and raffles can raise large amounts of money for your PAC, as well as generate good publicity. Such events are a great deal of work, so you must measure the project's cost in money and time against potential financial and public relations benefits. Make sure you have enough volunteers to do the work. Don't make the mistake of thinking that tickets to events or raffles will sell themselves. Try to have the costs of large dinners underwritten to ensure that the funds generated will go to help your local PAC and candidates.

*In-kind contributions* include office furniture and equipment, supplies, stamps, automobiles, labor, printing, and refreshments. Many states require in-kind contributions to be reported just like cash contributions. Establish the cash value of the donated object or service, and then formally declare it as a contribution.

*Direct mail* solicitation in large quantities should only be undertaken with the supervision of the appropriate PAC committee.

## Voter Registration Drives

You cannot vote for anyone unless you are registered. In most states you must be registered at least thirty days before an election. All the potential voters supporting your candidate must be registered. Recent reliable surveys have shown that only one-half of the average church congregation is registered to vote. That means that the other half—the nonregistered churchgoers—have neglected their citizen's right to elect moral public officials. The task of the PAC's voter registration chairperson is to register all the potential voters who will vote for your candidate. You can be sure your opponents are registering those who are likely to vote for them.

You need to inform yourself about the registration requirements in your state and county. The office of your county clerk or your supervisor of elections can answer the following questions:

- What are the residency requirements to vote (both state and county)? What happens to your registration when you change your address within a precinct? Within your county?
- Are there any additional requirements (e.g., for naturalized citizens or because of a change of name due to marriage)?
- Are you required to register by political party? In some states, you may have to declare party affiliation, which en-

titles you to vote both in that party's primary as well as in the general election. In other states, you merely register to vote, and then when you vote in a primary, you simply ask for the ballot of a particular party.

- How often does a voter need to reregister? In some states your registration lapses if you do not vote in several consecutive elections or if you move.

You will, of course, need to find out all the details of how you can organize a registration drive. The office of your county clerk or your supervisor of elections can provide answers to these questions:

- What is the deadline for registering to vote in the next election?
- Where can persons in your area register to vote? A printed list is often available showing the times and public places where deputy registrars are available. You can carry that list with you and advise all your candidate's supporters where to register and, if necessary, take them to register.
- Where can a person find helpful pamphlets or literature on voter registration drives and voting?

**Registration plan.** Your PAC should establish a plan to register all members of each participating church by districts. Recruit people through the CIAG coordinators and plan month-long registration drives.

Secure the cooperation of the pastor. If he approves of your plan and urges the congregation to register, your job is easy. The pastor may provide you with the membership list of the congregation. Some churches publish lists of the congregation, which are available to all members.

Set up a voter registration table at your church in the hall or foyer, if it is permitted in your county. Voters could register before and after services or special activities.

Ask your county clerk or elections supervisor if a PAC can set up its own tables to register voters.

Ask about the requirements necessary to deputize a person to register voters. You might become a deputy registrar yourself. Deputy (or floating) registrars are appointed by the county clerk or the supervisor of elections. If you know a deputy registrar you would prefer to have, you may request a specific individual. Precinct committee members are often deputy registrars in their precincts.

If the pastor will allow it, have ushers pass a voter's registration card to worshipers as they enter the Sunday service. Have the pastor announce that everyone should fill out the cards and place them in the offering plate. At the end of the service collect the cards and make copies. Try to do this two Sundays in a row in the spring and in the fall. This is a function for a CIAG.

**Suggestions for voter registration tables.** The registration must be nonpartisan. You must give Democrats, Republicans, and independents a chance to register. Do not display pictures and literature of candidates during voter registration drives at your church.

Put the registration table in a location where people will notice it. Make the table attractive and colorful. Have plenty of registration cards and ballpoint pens.

Make sure the deputy registrar is a friendly person. It is a good idea to have greeters at the door of the church directing people to the registration table. If people are not sure their registration is valid, register them again. Make a special effort to get eighteen-year-olds to register for the first time.

If regulations require church members to travel to some specified location in order to register, the registration drive will require more volunteers to assist the registration coordinator. When planning voter registration drives, be sure to recruit enough volunteers for transportation needs and baby-sitting requirements.

If your PAC's plan is going to be effective, it is necessary to have the ability to talk with each identified unregistered voter. Your church issues awareness group coordinator should have a telephone committee who can handle this project. If not, please recruit one immediately to help with that important program. The committee should have one volunteer caller for every fifty families.

After identifying unregistered voters, notify them as to when and where to register. Use all the ways possible within your church to do this, such as announcements in church and the church bulletin. Make sure the telephone committee is prepared. Remember, this is a special effort to register as many of your identified unregistered voters as possible. The CIAG registration coordinator and the pastor should assist at the registration location in any way they can.

All volunteers participating in the drive should know the location of registration sites, the days and hours the sites are open for registration, and the last day to register before an election.

During the registration drive the CIAG registration coordinator should call registration officials at least once a week to check their list of new people who have registered against the master list developed by the church. By the last week try to get each person not on the list to register.

## Campaign Materials and Supplies

In a campaign one of the keys to using grassroots volunteers effectively is to supply them with adequate materials and information. Each volunteer needs the resources and equipment to perform his or her assigned task. Campaign materials and supplies include:

- Three-inch by eight-and-a-half-inch cards on bond paper with information about the candidate on one side and his or her positions on issues on the reverse. Such cards are distributed during neighborhood walks.
- Pro-family voter report cards are essential for turning out the church vote, and should be nonpartisan and cover several issues showing how each candidate stands on each issue. The information on the report card may be from

voting records, candidate statements, media reports, or the candidate's position papers.

- Campaign signs don't have to be expensive to be effective. One-hundred-twenty-pound bond paper stapled to wooden cross stakes will last through most bad weather. The sign should use bright colors, be very visible, and not too wordy. The candidate's name and the office he or she is running for should be prominent. When putting the sign near a street, place three to five signs every hundred feet and around the entrance to the polling place.

- Campaign letters for bulk mailing can be developed with standard formats for recruiting volunteers, educating voters, raising funds, and informing pastors and business leaders of issues and events.

To save money, obtain a red political sticker from your post office to place on your bundles. Campaign bulk mail will then be treated as first-class mail. Go to your local post office for more details.

- Phone scripts should be typed and provided for the volunteers who call potential voters. The scripts should be clear, concise, and tailored for special-interest groups.

- Videos and audiotapes can be utilized by even the smallest campaign to get the candidate's message to volunteers and voters.

- Bumper stickers, report forms, donation envelopes, badges, and any other campaign supplies should also be available.

A volunteer provided with adequate resources will have confidence in a campaign's management and know his or her efforts are a needed asset to the campaign.

You will find that effectively planning a campaign with distinct and clearly defined titles and functions for staff will aid in winning a campaign. You may need to add or delete positions according to the size of the campaign, i.e., state or local.

You can organize, educate, phone, gather assets, names, or

computers, but if you do not implement a plan of action and timeline for the goal of electing people to office or of getting specific legislation passed, you are only half as effective as you could be.

# Implementing the Strategy

Every person involved in a campaign will be making contacts with potential voters. The following is a sample script that could be utilized by volunteers making telephone calls. Adjustments to the script can be made easily to fit the situation.

*Sample Script*

"Hello, my name is [name]. I know you from your involvement in [organization], and I'm working to elect [candidate] for [office].

"It is critically important that we elect such men and women on [election date] because . . .

"To do this, we are organizing a grassroots campaign. We need to enlist every possible person who is concerned about preserving our Judeo-Christian values. Will you be willing to help, even in a small way, to pass information along to a few friends?

"Let me tell you what else needs to be done, and you can tell me how you can help best. As you respond, I will make a note of what you would like to do so we can send you any materials you will need.

"Would you be willing to [activity]?" [Read every item on

the list. Explain that if each of us only does what we can comfortably do, the election will be a success.]

"Thank you for your assistance. Let's keep in touch."

## Sample Volunteer Form

As you are using your telephone script, you should always have a volunteer form at hand to keep accurate records. Your form can be changed to meet current needs.

Name of Volunteer             Date    Precinct #    Phone

---

Address _____ City _____ Zip _____

Received campaign contact from (neighbor, church, work, etc.) Be specific. _____

Church _____

I am willing to

( ) vote for _____.
( ) pray daily for the elections.
( ) phone to solicit support from my own church or neighborhood.
( ) walk in my neighborhood.
( ) walk in other assigned areas.
( ) have neighborhood coffee parties.
( ) recruit five other volunteers.
( ) donate   ( )$50   ( )$25   ( )$15.
( ) display a bumper sticker.

( ) display a yard sign.
( ) distribute bumper stickers.
( ) distribute yard signs.
( ) coordinate the work of ten other volunteers by relaying instructions (by phone) and distributing campaign material to them.

Please return form to:
PAC Campaign Chairperson
[address]

After the form is completed, explain that you will forward the form to PAC campaign headquarters so that the necessary information and materials will get to them.

## The Phone Bank

One of the best ways to help your PAC's candidates is to operate a phone bank. Because your PAC knows its members, you will be more effective and productive than most phone banks. The purpose of the phone bank is to

- call all registered Judeo-Christian voters for their support.
- determine how each voter called will vote and if he or she needs additional information.
- keep accurate records on potential favorable votes with file cards or by entering names in a computer. Doing so will assist the PAC's GOTV team on election day.
- persuade undecided voters that your candidate is best. Do this by sending literature through the mail. Never argue on the telephone.
- recruit volunteers to help with other PAC campaign activities.

Phone banks are run most successfully when several (perhaps a dozen) phones are located in the same place. Volunteers should work in two- or three-hour shifts under the personal direction of the PAC phone chairperson. All callers should use a similar script. Results should be tabulated every hour and at the end of each day.

Make the phoning fun. It is a tedious task, and the PAC phone chairperson should keep spirits and morale high among the volunteer callers. Train the callers to be courteous no matter what the response is on the other end of the phone. Have simple refreshments on hand.

The telephone solicitation strategy should be coordinated with the overall campaign strategy. If the initial calling proves to be counterproductive, you should reevaluate the calling technique and script for possible improvements before too much time is wasted.

Church issues awareness groups should have a phone team available. Divide the names in the church directory among the team and call church members, making a list of names, addresses, phone numbers, and precinct numbers of those giving favorable responses.

Here is an example of a script that PAC callers could use:

"[Mr./Mrs.] [name]. This is [your name]. I'm a volunteer for a PAC helping the [candidate's name] campaign for [office]. I am encouraged that we have a [man/woman] of ability, practical experience, and biblical convictions running for this [national/ state/county/city] office. First, I'd like to ask if we can count on your vote? [If the response is "yes," continue.]

"May I tell you some other things you can do to help?" [Read from the volunteer checklist and check what the person is willing to do.]

Here is an example of a shorter script that could be used on election day:

"[Mr./Mrs.] [name]. This is [your name]. I'm calling for [candidate's name] to remind you to please be sure to vote. It is going to be a tough race and your vote is crucial. Many thanks!"

Because you have worked hard to identify voters who may vote for PAC-supported candidates representing your values, don't lose them on election day.

An effective phone bank may determine whether a candidate wins. Diligent volunteers will know the community and be able to communicate the needs of the voters to the PAC directors and coordinators. A good phone solicitation team will keep accurate records and keep enthusiasm going into the home stretch.

*Neighborhood Walks*

The PAC walk chairperson coordinates all neighborhood walks in the primary and general elections. The first neighborhood walk should attempt to identify the voters, recruit volunteers, gather pertinent demographic data, and register or arrange to register favorable voters.

The second neighborhood walk should attempt to turn out the vote and should be made two days prior to the election. The best days to walk are Monday, Tuesday, and Thursday from 5:30 P.M. to 9:00 P.M. and on Saturday from 10:00 A.M. to 1:00 P.M. Volunteer walkers should find at least 76 percent of the people at home during those times.

The walk chairperson should hold a training session two months prior to each election in order to give the phone bank committee time to use the collected information for campaign purposes. Schedule volunteers to arrive for training at headquarters in a group. It is suggested that walkers in one group not exceed sixty individuals. PACs in cities that plan to walk in five precincts or less will require only one group to train. PACs that plan to walk in more than five precincts may require more than one group of volunteers.

## NEIGHBORHOOD WALK
## PRECINCT CANVASS WORKSHEET

Precinct #_____ Worker _____ Date: _____

| # STREET/ AVENUE | VOTER NAME | PRIMARY | STATUS | TELEPHONE NUMBER |
|---|---|---|---|---|
|  |  |  |  |  |
|  |  |  |  |  |

*Instructions for Volunteer Walkers*

The PAC neighborhood walk trainer should give the following instructions to volunteer walkers:

- House or apartment numbers and street names should be recorded in the appropriate columns of the precinct canvass worksheet (see above).
- If there is no response to the doorbell or to knocking, indicate no response under the status column of the precinct canvass worksheet and leave campaign literature at the door. (Do not place literature in mail boxes). Go immediately to the next house.

If there is a response, the following script could be used:

"Hello, my name is [your name]. I am a volunteer. Are there any [candidate's name] supporters in your household?" [Record response and continue script.] If the election were held today would you support [your candidate's name] or [opposing candidate's name]? [Record the response.]

- If undecided or nonsupporters, hand them campaign literature and thank them for their time. Go immediately to the next house.

- If people are supporters, record their names, telephone numbers, and church.
- Find out whether supporters of PAC-supported candidates are registered to vote.
- If supporters are not registered give the supporters voter registration cards.
- Ask whether the supporter can help as a volunteer in the campaign.
- If supporters want to help in the campaign, indicate that fact on the precinct canvass worksheet. Give them the appropriate campaign literature and go immediately to the next house.
- In order to contact the maximum number of favorable voters, do *not* get involved in lengthy discussions.

### Sample Follow-up Letters

Following are some sample letters I have used in campaigns. You should personalize the letters you use. You may find that you need scripts and letters with different wording for each cluster grouping.

Construct your letters to be easy to read and clear in their message that have as their objective getting volunteers or donations.

When you have volunteers to construct your correspondence, make it clear to them what you expect them to do, how to do it, and where to obtain the necessary tools and information to accomplish the task. Don't overload volunteers—you can give them more after they have completed the initial task.

*Dear Friend,*

*This letter is to announce the opening of the campaign headquarters of [candidate's name]. We have campaign literature and materials available for you to distribute through your club or organization.*

*We are receiving many volunteers from churches and Christian organizations throughout the county who could be of help in this precinct.*

*If you personally are interested in helping [candidate's name] become the next Republican [title of office], please call us. We need your help and ability.*

*We are looking forward to victory in November!*

*Dear Phone Volunteer,*

*Thank you so much for offering to telephone potential voters from your own home for the [candidate's name] campaign. You are going to have a very important part in helping win this election.*

*Please begin calling people right away. If you do not have an assigned list of names, please let us know and we will provide one for you.*

*We are enclosing an effective telephone script for you to use, as well as information on [candidate's name] and a fact sheet that you can refer to when people ask specific questions. To save time, go over this information before you begin calling.*

*We are also sending you five volunteer information forms. Feel free to duplicate more, if more people are willing to become involved.*

*We will be having a training session for all telephone callers on [date], and we would like you to attend. Please let me know if you have any questions. [signed, PAC phone chairperson]*

*Dear Friend,*

*Friendship and involvement is what this letter is all about.*

*The campaign to elect [candidate's name] has been gaining momentum all over the state. That is not due to the amount of money spent on mass media, but because individuals are telling their friends about our convocations and goals.*

*We need an army of volunteers in the final month who can work together to insure that every neighborhood, town, and county hears our message. We feel that message is best delivered from neighbor to neighbor, church member to church member, and from friend to friend.*

*We ask you to make five or more copies of the enclosed volunteer interest form and ask five or more friends to join our efforts. Please return the completed forms to us as soon as possible.*

*We are looking forward to victory in November!*

# The Use of Postcards

Postcards provide an inexpensive means of imprinting the candidate's name in the voter's mind. However, they do not provide space for an in-depth analysis of the issues or even an outline of your candidate's credentials. For that reason, postcards are effectively used to announce candidate endorsements.

Postcards are particularly useful when sent by people to their own friends. When your good friend or neighbor tells you John Doe is a good candidate and asks you to vote for him, this is a personal recommendation, and most people respond positively. You might have a postcard party of friends and church members to prepare postcards. The cards can be sent to the members of the church, civic clubs, or to people on lists supplied by the PAC.

### Sample Postcard

*Dear [name],*

*I wanted to let you know I'm supporting John Doe for state senate. After studying the candidates and their positions, I'm convinced that John will best represent our community.*

*P.S. Call me for more information or a scorecard of all the candidates.*

# Endorsements

If voters don't know the candidate personally, they may look to see who his friends are. Most people have some faith in the old adages "a man is known by the company he keeps" and "birds of a feather flock together."

The candidates your PAC supports, then, should seek the endorsement of Christian leaders who are prominent, well-liked, and credible. Pastors, civic leaders, and prominent citizens can influence a great many votes by publicly endorsing your candidate. Such endorsements make excellent news releases. For example, a neighborhood organization could endorse the candidate, because he or she has a firm stand against littering, or a Christian school principal could mention your candidate's favorable position on private schools. Your local taxpayers' association or city council member could praise your candidate for helping to keep taxes down.

You can increase your news coverage of endorsements by organizing events in connection with the endorsement. A picture of your candidate receiving an important endorsement while attending a church dinner would make a good newspaper photo.

### Sample News Release

From JOHN DOE-FOR-SENATE HQRS. FOR IMMEDIATE RELEASE

The [name of PAC], a local political action committee, announced today their endorsement of John Doe for state representative.

[Name], president of [name of PAC], said, "John has faithfully represented the people of his district for the last six years. He has voted every year for lower taxes, and he has a consistent record of conservative handling of taxpayers' money. We're proud to endorse his candidacy for reelection. He is a strong supporter of family values and is anti-abortion.

"We are going to do all we can," said [name], "to get John elected in November."

John Doe previously has received the endorsements of [e.g. the policemen's association, the league of Christian voters, and the homeowners taxpayer's association].

## Surveys and Polls

Many candidates will have expenses available for surveying their constituents. Surveying and polling can be very important to the outcome of an election. Your PAC can provide a valuable service to its candidate by finding out how the voters think about one or more of the issues. Conducting surveys will also enable your PAC to stay in tune with the public.

PAC-conducted polling may be accomplished by different methods, such as the use of automatic dialing machines, phone banks, or direct mailings. You will be able to use those methods to reach people on voter registration lists. Survey questions can also be distributed at the churches by members of the church issues awareness group.

The Christian community is as diversified as the secular community. For example, Christians with lower incomes may have different interests and viewpoints than those with higher incomes.

Survey committees also have a very positive influence on the growth and success of your PAC. If the PAC is to represent the entire Christian community, then it must know the needs and concerns of every Christian.

When preparing survey questions, eliminate as much biased language as possible. Do not assume your PAC knows the interests of the Christian community. Do not assume the Christian community knows the voting record of an incumbent or a candidate's personal lifestyle.

## The Media

Most of the Christian voters in your district may never meet your candidate. They will know him or her only through the eyes and ears of the media or through the information you provide. The media image the candidate develops may influence more voters than personal appearances and contacts. That image, therefore, must accurately reflect the candidate's integrity, sincerity, concern for the voters, and positions on key issues.

To assess how the media may be used by your PAC, take a *media inventory*. Make a detailed, written evaluation of all the media resources in the area, that is, all the television and radio stations, newspapers, religious publications, union newsletters, and other publications. The newspaper, radio, or television station with the greatest influence may be based outside the district but widely heard or read within the district.

Create a *news media evaluation sheet* on which you list current information about each media outlet, such as its correct name and business address and telephone number. Find out who political editors are and their deadline days and times.

Make up a *press kit*. The PAC media chairperson should present every newspaper editor and television and radio station manager with a press kit. The press kit should be a folder containing information that gives a concise but complete view of your PAC or the candidate you are promoting. A plain folder from the local stationery store with a bumper sticker on the front will do the job.

The press kit could include

- a black and white glossy photo of your candidate with the PAC county director. Other photos showing the candidate interacting with the people of the community could be included.
- a biography of the candidate emphasizing a conservative voting record if he or she is an officeholder or qualifications if the candidate is seeking office for the first time.
- information on your PAC.
- the candidate's statement announcing his or her candidacy and the first news release, which could be the PAC's endorsement.
- any other news releases that are important to the theme of the campaign, such as one stating the candidate's position on crime or taxes.
- a sample of the candidate's campaign material, such as brochures, bumper stickers, buttons, or the PAC's material endorsing the candidate.
- names, addresses, and phone numbers of the PAC chairperson, campaign manager, and headquarters.
- a letter from the candidate on official campaign stationery addressed to the editor or news director stating that the candidate has announced his or her candidacy and hopes

soon to have the pleasure of a meeting. Such a letter should be short, simple, and sincere.

## Developing Media Knowledge

After you have made your survey of information and prepared enough press kits, the PAC county chairperson and the media chairperson should make a personal call on the editor of every newspaper and the news director of every television and radio station. District directors could meet with the editors of small newspapers. Such meetings could be the most important interviews your PAC or candidate has during the entire campaign. If a newspaper, television, or radio station is a large one, make an appointment in advance.

Many candidates and PAC members have made the mistake of thinking that a newspaper editor already knows the issues, voting records, and personalities. However, your PAC or candidate is only one of a thousand potential news items. It is your responsibility to make it easy for the editor to know the favorable facts about your candidate and the positions he or she takes.

PAC representatives should also meet with the following media contacts: street reporters at area television stations, the directors of evening news programs and interview programs, and local personalities such as hosts of talk shows.

When interviews with reporters or editors are over, be careful of the off-the-record remark. Many a candidate has been ruined by a careless remark. Media professionals can be your friends or your enemies, but it is their job to get a story to sell papers or create programming. Remember, a good reporter never quits working.

## News Conferences

1. Never schedule a news conference later than 2:30 P.M. After that it's old news and may be ignored. Noon is a good time.

2. Send out news conference announcements two or three days in advance. Then remind media representatives the day be-

fore the conference. If the candidate is a pro-family candidate, it may be harder to get coverage, so work for it.

3. Reserve the room for the news conference ahead of time.

4. Mark off a special section for television cameras, or you may find them blocking everyone's view.

5. Have your PAC county director and the candidate in the front of the room where microphones can be placed.

6. Start your news conference on time. Have a PAC spokesperson ready if the candidate hasn't arrived. The spokesperson can begin the news conference to hold the attention of the reporters.

7. The PAC media chairperson should begin the conference by introducing the candidate with two or three sentences only. The candidate should give a prepared statement of about five minutes. Then allow the reporters to ask questions.

8. Mail or hand-carry press releases to the offices of media representatives who did not attend.

### Preparation for Press Releases

Make your PAC press releases based on a biblical perception of the issues and include supporting evidence. Don't be overly religious in your wording or use many Scripture references. Recruit spokespersons for the PAC who are influential and who communicate well and with tact in public. A news conference is not a time for confrontation but an opportunity to distribute press releases and make the PAC's positions known. Remember, there were Daniels and there were Elijahs; use your gifts in the proper place at the proper time. Don't let the media discredit you because of irrational or uninformed statements.

Make the press conference newsworthy with press releases on issues, statements challenging the opposition, appointments of key figures in the campaign, and endorsements by prominent leaders.

Media time is valuable and many candidates may be vying for a few minutes on the nightly news. Plan your media events to be the best. Be prepared with press releases that get attention.

*Events for Your Candidate*

When I started in politics, I was taught to look for creative ways to take the candidate to the people.

- Take the candidate to speak at special functions, such as fairs, store openings, and graduations.
- Plan events where people gather, such as malls or the courthouse.
- Choose a fitting backdrop for your candidate's speech, such as the site of a project of your candidate's that was well received; or, for example, have the candidate speak about crime in front of the jail or courthouse.
- The candidate could attend pro-life rallies or visit large churches.

*Media Advertising*

The purposes of campaign advertising are
- get voters to vote for your candidate.
- deliver pro-family and traditional-values voters for your candidate.
- expose the negative qualities of your opponent.
- get candidates to discuss and commit themselves to positions on your PAC's political agenda.

*What Are Your Media Options?*

What media options are affordable for the average PAC campaign? Don't make a mistake and believe print advertising is always less costly than television. Listed below are four helpful guidelines for deciding what advertising options are the most advantageous.

1. Ask media marketing directors for political rates. The media is required by law to give your PAC or candidate the lowest rate it has charged any customer during the past year.

2. Television spots lasting thirty or sixty seconds can be produced for under one thousand dollars. Computer graphics can be utilized for special effects.

3. Radio spots lasting thirty or sixty seconds should cost between fifty dollars and one hundred dollars to produce. Some radio stations will write and produce the ad free of charge if you buy time from them.

4. Cable television public access ads should cost under two hundred fifty dollars to produce a thirty-second spot and under five hundred dollars to produce a sixty-second spot.

Richard Armstrong, the author of *The Next Hurrah* (must reading for political activists), describes how one state assemblyman utilized cable television programs to beat an incumbent. The candidate produced thirty-minute programs using a town meeting format to present his positions. The programs cost a fraction of what his opponent paid affiliated network stations for ads during prime time. The prime time ads reached many more voters, but most were out of the voting area and could not vote in the election.

Your PAC should be able to purchase time for two-minute ads with most cable networks for under $120. A two-minute segment gives your PAC or candidate an excellent opportunity to present the positions taken on central issues.

Using network-affiliated television stations can be an affordable option if you target a specific audience. Airing campaign ads during late-night movies, early morning news, Christian programs, and women's magazine programs will reach large numbers of Christian and conservative voters. Generally, such air times are less expensive than programming during prime time. These time placements will cost between twenty-five and one hundred dollars per thirty-second spot. I have used these in several races to be able to get affordable television spots.

## Coffee Parties and Videos

The coffee party is an excellent forum for showing campaign videos to neighborhood groups, home prayer groups, and Bible study groups. The television and the videotape player continues to play a major role in campaigns. Currently, 75 percent of American homes have VCRs.

The use of videotapes will allow your candidate to be in many places at once, speak on a variety of issues, and assist in motivating volunteers with a personal message.

## A Candidate Who Used Coffee Parties

In 1987 I consulted for Warren Lark, a retired pastor who decided to run for mayor of Kirby, Texas, a city of ten thousand and a suburb of San Antonio.

His first venture into politics, Warren's natural thought was to pay for and manage the campaign himself. I told him to reconsider, and said he was cheating friends out of the joy and blessing of being a part of his campaign. I advised him to set up a campaign committee and follow a plan.

We also reviewed his political assets.

1. He had the endorsement of many civic leaders.
2. Several incumbent councilmen encouraged him to run.
3. He had an excellent reputation and was well known in the community.
4. He knew how to relate to people from his experiences in the military and from serving as a pastor for fourteen years.

Listed below are some of the actions Warren took to build a campaign.

1. He formed a small campaign steering committee.
2. He established a campaign fund and had donation envelopes printed.
3. He opened a campaign headquarters in a small building behind his house.
4. He organized volunteers who solicited support by telephone from their homes.
5. He obtained a list of registered voters and campaigned door-to-door, stopping only at the homes of registered voters.
6. He organized neighborhood coffee parties.

As a result of these efforts Mayor Lark won the election with over 60 percent of the votes and spent less than two thousand dollars.

## Setting Up Coffee and Video Parties

1. Contact the candidate to find if the candidate will be available in person and if not how to obtain a campaign videotape.

2. Recruit a host or hostess for coffee parties in each voting area.

3. Have the phone bank volunteers invite voters to come. The voters who attend should live in the same neighborhood.

4. Coffee parties should be hosted by people who are leaders, trend setters, and have a suitable home.

5. Coffee parties should be planned to have standing room only. Invite one hundred people if you want twenty-five to attend.

One person should coordinate PAC-sponsored coffee parties, so that a candidate's staff can communicate with the same person about details and the same person can drive the candidate to the coffee parties if more than one is scheduled in a day.

Supporters who host coffee parties should be willing to

- open their homes to as many as fifty people.
- make a list of friends and neighbors and invite them.
- prepare refreshments.
- be sure all volunteer interest forms and donations collected during the party are sent to PAC headquarters.
- have available a videotape player.
- greet guests and serve refreshments (allow twenty minutes).
- introduce the candidate or videotape.
- ask for campaign donations and volunteers.

Don't take anything for granted when organizing a coffee party. Have an agenda and stick to it.

# Election Day

The PAC election day committee and election day coordinator are essential to a campaign. Every effort should be made to get out the vote.

## The Election Day Coordinator

The election day coordinator monitors all activities during the campaign. Everyone should understand that in the five days before election day, every coordinator and chairperson comes under his or her supervision. Because the election day coordinator needs to have the maximum number of volunteers and broadest coverage possible, do not stop recruiting volunteers until the day before the election. All volunteers should notify the election coordinator of their needs on a daily basis. Election day coordinators should keep in mind the following tasks and goals:

1. The last campaign-related mailing should be planned to arrive at voters' homes the day before or the day of the election to inform them of any late-breaking news and polls.

2. Letters to the editor and press releases should be increased the last three weeks prior to election day to coincide with paid publicity.

3. All phone bank volunteers should have a copy of a list of registered voters to call and use a script that encourages people to vote.

4. All election-related notices included in church bulletins should be at the church a week prior to election day.

5. All election day poll workers should be trained to gather and report polling site developments.

6. On election day phone banks at PAC headquarters should be verifying all volunteer activity. Election day is a hectic time, and the election day coordinator must monitor all PAC-related efforts.

7. Election day coordinators should be sure that officials of the political party you are assisting, the candidate's staff, and other PAC members are aware of one another's activities. If possible share information and materials.

8. Encourage Christian fellowship among volunteers to help keep a rejoicing, happy atmosphere. No matter the outcome of the election, the victor is the Lord, and we should be doing His work.

9. Always set reasonable goals for your workers on election day. Do not overwork volunteers early in the day, and do not overuse the same volunteers. The PAC volunteer coordinator and election day coordinator should meet a week prior to election day to review and plan work assignments.

## Vote Goals

Your candidate's objective is to receive at least 51 percent of the votes cast on election day. The vote goal for each precinct is not, however, necessarily 51 percent of the votes cast in each precinct. Some precincts will be more favorable to your candidate, some to your opponent. Some precincts are more Republican, some more Democratic. Based on previous similar elections, the vote goal is an estimated but realistic figure of how many votes your candidate can get in each precinct.

The PAC's campaign committee will refer to your PAC's voting pattern and demographic data, and they will figure the vote goals for each precinct. PAC precinct coordinators should not try to work out the vote goals for their own precincts.

Determining vote goals for a district requires

- a study of actual election returns (by precinct) in two or three previous elections.
- political judgment and knowledge to determine what variables may change voting patterns in the next election.
- a willingness to do tedious work with figures.

Often two or three PAC members can work together to make up the precinct vote goals for a district. The variables will include whether the previous elections were affected by a presidential, gubernatorial or senatorial race; whether your candidate had stiff opposition in previous elections; and whether many new people have moved into the district. Figuring vote goals can be a key to preparing for your candidate's victory.

The PAC can obtain election information for determining precinct vote goals from the following sources:

- county clerk
- board of elections
- registrar of voters
- county chairperson of a political party
- public library
- state secretary of state
- local newspaper

Consider the following questions when determining precinct vote goals:

- Is the data from a presidential election year?
- Has your candidate run before?
- Were controversial issues on the ballot or other strong candidates of similar views—coattail effect?
- Has the population increased or decreased significantly?
- What is the socioeconomic status of voters in each precinct?
- How stable is the conservative vote?
- Do vote totals for Bush from 1988 show the potential conservative vote in each precinct?

Be sure you have calculated enough votes to win. Do not overestimate your precinct vote goals, or you will discourage precinct workers. You only need 51 percent of the vote to win.

## Getting-Out-the-Vote

It is unfortunate but true that approximately one-half of all Americans do not vote on election day. People need all the encouragement possible, and sometimes help and assistance, if they are to vote.

The most effective way to provide that encouragement, or to identify those who need assistance, is by using the telephone. In many churches an established telephone committee can be utilized; in others such a committee should be established.

The church phone bank (nonpartisan) can be sponsored or organized by the church issues awareness group. Other phone committees should be organized to contact voters not on church lists. Lists should be divided so that no one person has more than twenty calls to make, unless he or she agrees to call more.

The first call should be made the night before the election. The purpose of the call is to

- remind voters that the following day is election day and, if at all possible, to vote early.
- remind voters to study a sample ballot and encourage them to review the list of PAC-supported candidates.
- determine if anyone in the household needs assistance, such as a baby sitter or transportation. If so, that name should be given to the person coordinating that kind of assistance.

The second call should be made midday on election day to determine if they have voted yet. If so, thank them and cross their names from the list. If not, remind them how important their vote is and that typically there is no waiting at the polls during the afternoon.

The third and final call should be made about ninety minutes before the polls close to all the people whose names were not crossed off during the second call. Again, the message is the same: thanks if they have voted and encouragement to do so if they haven't.

On election day our first priority is to turn out voters with

Judeo-Christian traditional values. Get-out-the-vote programs on a much broader scale are run by candidates of both parties with the big difference being that they don't care who is voting for them as long as they get enough votes to win. Get-out-the-vote programs run through churches can deliver the Christian votes for the PAC-supported candidate. After the election, it will be easy to show that candidate how he or she won. Perhaps as a newly elected official the candidate will exercise a greater level of commitment to traditional moral values.

## Poll Watchers and Workers

Even in well-publicized elections, up to 8 percent of the voters are undecided, and in lesser known elections it can be as high as 60 percent. Thus, the election day coordinator should decide whether volunteers should be assigned to sit or stand outside the polling place with campaign literature all day on election day.

Remember, there can be no electioneering within one hundred feet of the polls, which will be marked by the election judge. This may vary in each state, so check with your local election administrator. You *can* pass out several candidates' campaign materials, if you comply with regulations governing partisan activities on election day.

## Absentee Ballots

Absentee ballots have often been enough to swing a close election, and it is important that your candidate not lose favorable votes because some of his or her supporters will be out of town on election day. There are two types of absentee voters—absentee by mail and absentee in person. Absentee voters are more important today than ten years ago, because many states have changed absentee laws. Absentee voters may include businesspeople making trips, military personnel, college students, and others. Find out the procedure for absentee voting and advise all PAC precinct coordinators. In some states the voter must apply for the absentee ballot a couple of weeks before the election so that the county clerk has time to mail the ballot, and the voter has time to return it. In many states the PAC can get a list of people who have applied for an absentee ballot in previous elections. Volunteers can go to the county clerk's office and copy the names and addresses of absentee voters onto envelopes with letters from your candidate asking them to vote. That is a very effective campaign tactic, because every letter will go to someone who is already planning to vote. You may assign this list to a caller to assist the absentee voter.

Find out whether incapacitated voters (in nursing homes, for example) use absentee ballots or a different procedure. Such voters can represent a sizable number of votes for your candidate.

## Operation Doorknob

One of the last activities of your PAC's part in an election plan begins at 5:00 A.M. on election day.

Operation Doorknob consists of volunteers placing voting reminder cards on doorknobs of every voter in each precinct who has pledged a vote for your candidate. Imagine the favorable impression the voters will have when they find a flier on their doorknobs as they leave for work or go to get the morning paper. The doorknob cards can be attractive cardboard with a string loop to hang over the knob. They should contain a short printed message from your candidate reminding the residents that their vote is needed. They can contain a simple message: GOOD MORNING! IT'S ELECTION DAY. TIME TO VOTE FOR [CANDIDATE'S NAME]. If Operation Doorknob is not possible, mail a reminder telling the voters where their polling place is. Again, your PAC should be concerned with the voters identified as Judeo-Christian traditional-values supporters.

It takes fewer volunteers than we realize to win an election and enough committed volunteers can make up for a lack of funds. From working in campaigns and from studies produced by the different parties, I have found these estimates:

- Fifty percent of evangelicals are registered and only 50 percent of those vote.

- In a presidential election 52 percent of the registered voters turn out to vote.
- In a statewide election 40 percent to 45 percent of the registered voters vote.
- In a city election 30 percent to 35 percent of the registered voters vote.
- In a school board election only 4 percent to 5 percent of the registered voters vote.

## The Campaign Calendar

The importance of a detailed campaign calendar should not be underestimated. To create the calendar start with election day activities and work backward. Put all aspects of the campaign on the calendar: media events, surveys, special events, party precinct meetings, volunteer and fund-raising goals, direct mailing schedules, literature production plans, and so forth. As you place the various items on the calendar, the campaign plan will become clear. The calendar provides a means by which campaign operations can be visualized and worked out before problems arise. Coordinating events, deadlines, and goals can take place through the process of establishing and updating the campaign calendar. A review of a comprehensive campaign calendar provides an automatic check on all aspects of the campaign. If you don't have a campaign calendar, you don't have a campaign.

## Building for Victory

If you have built a good PAC precinct organization, it will be based on the following rules:

1. The PAC campaign coordinators must have determined precisely *who* is going to vote.

2. The get-out-the-vote program should enable the PAC to contact all voters who previously were identified as supporters before the election.

3. The election day coordinator must know by 3:00 P.M. to 5:00 P.M. of election day who of their favorable voters has not yet voted.

4. The election day precinct volunteers must then contact those voters and get them to the polls, offering assistance when necessary.

Those four points actually constitute the basis of GOTV.

On election day the get-out-the-vote program should be in place so that each PAC precinct chairperson can know how far short of the vote goal he or she is so that the time before the polls close can be used to turn out the needed voters.

## Ultimate Victory

We must realize that to rule we must first serve. In some states and counties the religious right in zealous fury took over the Republican party structure, only to find it did not have the expertise to run the party. Such an outcome could be disastrous, for it is the strength and proper use of the party system that elects candidates to office. If your group has the votes to be a 51 to 60 percent majority, then allow others with political expertise who may not share your ideology on all issues to serve.

Be not mistaken. Rules, laws, and politicians will not have the ultimate victory or succeed in turning a nation or world toward its Creator. Collective prayer and hearts humble before God bring repentance and revival to a nation.

We *must* participate in the political process, but we *must* also remember: "If My people who are called by My name will humble themselves, and pray and seek My face, and turn from their wicked ways, then I will hear from heaven, and will forgive their sin and heal their land" (2 Chron. 7:14).

# A Glossary of Political Offices

The following is a glossary of political offices based on elected positions in most states. These same offices may have different names in other states but usually serve similar functions.

Your organization can be involved in electing candidates for many offices. What follows are a few examples. Remember that power is local. To be a U.S. congressman is a noble goal, but not if it is an unreasonable goal due to a lack of knowledge and assets.

Many U.S. congressmen and U.S. senators started as local county commissioners, school board members, or state representatives. Out of the 435 U.S. congressmen, you will find very few who did not serve in some locally elected position before running for a higher office. This holds true for governors, lieutenant governors, attorneys general, or other statewide office.

There are many boards or positions in your community where you can serve and learn. Most local elections do not require many votes to win.

Your state may have open primary elections for office. Open primary elections occur when the Democrats or Republicans don't have separate primaries but rather choose the candidate

☆ **185** ☆

their party is endorsing in senatorial or congressional caucuses. The candidates then run. There may be two party-endorsed candidates, but there also may be several other candidates running as Democrats or Republicans without the party endorsement along with independent candidates. In these cases, unless one candidate gets 51 percent, the top two candidates face each other in a runoff.

*attorney general:* In most states, the attorney general is appointed by the governor to be the state's chief legal officer. In your state this may be an elected position. Annual salary ranges from $50,000 to $75,000.

*city council:* The city council governs municipalities. Its duties are to disburse the budget for the city, pass taxes, pass ordinances, and oversee implementation of local, state, and federal grants and programs.

*community action agency:* These community-based agencies were created in 1963 by President Johnson to disburse federal funds for programs targeting the elderly, the illiterate, emergency needs, and the poor. An agency official is elected to serve a two-year term on a board made up of one-third representatives of the poor, one-third other county or city officials, and one-third from organizations serving the community (this group is voted on by the first two). The representative of the poor is elected in an official election. Then each board will disburse funds for such programs as meals-on-wheels, housing for the homeless, job training, and many others. This is a special elected board to serve on and is established to develop relationships with the poor, minorities, and elderly.

*community college boards:* Such a board is elected by district. It oversees the budget and management of the community college in the district.

*county commissioner:* This local office is important because it is the foundation for county self-rule. Normally, the county is divided into fairly equal population districts with a commissioner elected to represent the people of that district. Collectively, county commissioners are responsible for the budgets of their districts, including expenditures for roads, sewers, general building, and maintenance. They may also set the budget for the justice of the peace and oversee disbursement of state and federal grants and programs.

*county judge:* This office is the magistrate of the board of county commissioners. The position holds influence over the budget of each county commissioner and in the disbursement of state and federal grants and program. They are the focal points of county self rule. Salary can range from $50,000 to $80,000.

*county sheriff:* This person is one of the most influential law enforcement officers in the county. Annual salary ranges from $25,000 to $50,000.

*governor:* This is usually a four-year term. The governor has a vast area of appointments and oversees budgets. In some states the governor can appoint the attorney general and secretary of state. Annual salary ranges from $50,000 to $75,000 plus expenses.

*public school board:* This is usually a two-year term. The member of the school board oversees the local school system and approves the budget, teacher raises, curriculum, and books. Expenses are usually reimbursed, but no salary is paid.

*soil and water board:* This four-year term is a very influential position. This board is usually elected by district voters. The member of the soil and water board approves development plans for subdivisions, city expansion, and water routes.

*state lieutenant governor:* This office is a four-year term and in most states is elected. The lieutenant governor serves as president of the senate and makes legislative committee appointments. Annual salary usually ranges from $50,000 to $70,000.

*state representative:* This office is a two-year term. The state representative writes legislation and has a budget for staff. Most states pay minimal amounts while the house of representatives is in session.

*state school board:* This is usually a four-year term. The member of the state school board oversees the state education

# Appendix A

agency, selects school books, approves curriculum, and approves the budget. Usually expenses are reimbursed, but no salary is paid.

*state senator:* This office is a four-year term. The state senator writes legislation and oversees the state budget. The state senator usually has a substantial budget for staff; pay differs from state to state.

*U.S. congressman:* This office is a two-year term. The congressman proposes legislation, including governmental expenditures. He approves or disapproves the official action of declaration of war. Salary usually begins at $125,000 with an average staff budget of $500,000 to $1,000,000.

*U.S. senator:* This is a six-year term. There are two senators from each state elected on a statewide basis. The U.S. senator passes legislation, with the exception of the spending bill, ratifies treaties, ratifies virtually all levels of appointments—U.S. attorney, Supreme Court, cabinet, military officers. Annual salary is $98,400. The average office budget ranges from $750,000 for a small state to $2,000,000 for a large state.

# An Overview of Party Convention Procedures

Selection of delegates to the party's national convention is governed by the state election code and by the rules of the state and national parties.

The state convention is composed of delegates selected at the party's county and senatorial district conventions and may be held on the second Saturday after the general primary. County and state senatorial district delegates are selected at the precinct conventions, which are held following the closing of the general primary polls. This may vary in your state, so obtain a copy of the rules from your party's state office.

The party precinct chairpersons are elected by the people. The chairpersons then will have a board, which will control party functions.

### Senatorial District Convention

Delegates to the state senatorial district conventions usually elect the members of a temporary nominations committee to be members of the permanent nominating committee. Those committees submit for approval a list of delegates and alternates to

# GOP STATE AND NATIONAL
# CONVENTION STRUCTURE

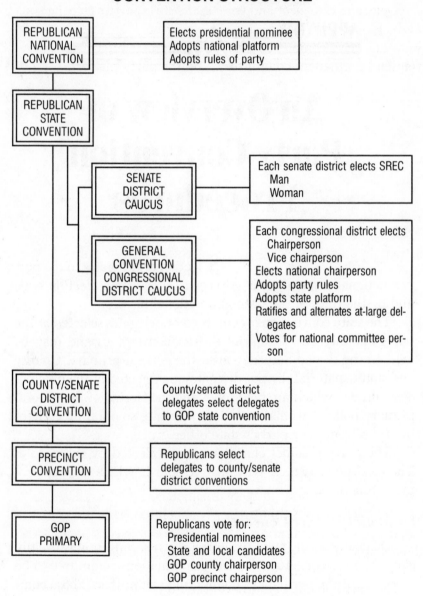

| | |
|---|---|
| REPUBLICAN NATIONAL CONVENTION | Elects presidential nominee<br>Adopts national platform<br>Adopts rules of party |
| REPUBLICAN STATE CONVENTION | |
| SENATE DISTRICT CAUCUS | Each senate district elects SREC<br>   Man<br>   Woman |
| GENERAL CONVENTION CONGRESSIONAL DISTRICT CAUCUS | Each congressional district elects<br>   Chairperson<br>   Vice chairperson<br>Elects national chairperson<br>Adopts party rules<br>Adopts state platform<br>Ratifies and alternates at-large delegates<br>Votes for national committee person |
| COUNTY/SENATE DISTRICT CONVENTION | County/senate district delegates select delegates to GOP state convention |
| PRECINCT CONVENTION | Republicans select delegates to county/senate district conventions |
| GOP PRIMARY | Republicans vote for:<br>   Presidential nominees<br>   State and local candidates<br>   GOP county chairperson<br>   GOP precinct chairperson |

# Convention Procedures

the state party convention. Delegates of the senatorial district convention approve or disapprove the list by majority vote. In the larger conventions, however, this approval is usually automatic.

Delegates also elect and vote on the state party's chairperson and vice-chairperson, national committee man and woman, state executive committee members, members of the state convention's permanent committees, and the party platform.

## The Party Precinct Convention

The purpose of the party precinct convention is to elect delegates and alternates to the senatorial district or county convention, which would be held two weeks after the primary. Resolutions would also be passed at precinct convention on various issues to be sent on to the senatorial district convention. The delegates and alternates chosen would go to the state convention. Those delegates and alternates would carry with them the resolutions that had been passed. If those resolutions are passed at the state convention, they would be adopted by the Republican party as its platform.

## The Party Precinct Chairperson Vs. Chairperson of the Precinct Convention

The party precinct chairperson is elected by the voters of a specific precinct to represent them on the county executive board of their party. Duties may vary some, but usually include sitting on the county executive board, helping register new voters in their precinct, assisting party candidates by organizing their precinct, keeping party members of their precinct informed about party business, and acting as an election judge or choosing the election judges at polls in their precinct.

The chairperson of the precinct convention is elected to manage the precinct convention. The chairperson's duties begin with the opening of the precinct convention and end with the closing of the precinct convention.

The party precinct chairperson could be elected chairperson

of the precinct convention, but the party precinct chairperson serves as the precinct chairperson of the convention only if elected to do so by the delegates to the convention.

Incumbent party precinct chairpersons may try to intimidate delegates to a precinct convention by assuming the position of temporary chairperson, acting as if they automatically become chairperson of the convention. However, such political maneuvers do not follow established party rules.

## Responsibilities of a Precinct Chairperson

The political parties traditionally have taken pride in their grassroots political strategy. Grassroots politics succeeds when every precinct chairperson has organized his or her precinct and carried out all of his or her responsibilities.

The precinct chairperson's primary responsibilities are to
- know the voters in the precinct by keeping accurate historical records of registered voters and voting patterns.
- find unregistered Republicans and have them register to vote.
- know all the Republican activists in the precinct.
- recruit interested Republicans to work in party activities.
- help GOP candidates hold campaign activities, and distribute literature and yard signs in the precinct.
- organize get-out-the-vote activities to insure that all Republican voters go to the polls on election day.
- attend all meetings of the county party's executive committee.
- call to order the Republican precinct convention as temporary precinct convention chairperson.

How important is it to organize a precinct? Always remember that every vote is important, and that, for example, some of the most important Republican victories in Texas were won by only a few votes per precinct! In the 1988 election for Texas Supreme Court, the candidate won by twenty thousand votes— three votes per precinct.

# Convention Procedures

### *How to Become the Party Precinct Chairperson*

One of the most influential positions in local politics is the precinct chairperson of a party. That is where the political influence and structure begin and is one of the easiest elected positions to win. In each precinct it normally requires two hundred or fewer votes. To begin a plan of action leading to obtaining the precinct chairperson position

- call the local party's headquarters and request an application for filing for precinct chairperson.
- request the name, address, and telephone number of the present precinct chairperson.
- call the present chairperson and find out his or her positions on the issues.
- obtain a list of the registered voters in your precinct (available from party headquarters).
- obtain a map of the precinct.
- call the county clerk's office and request a list of all the people who voted in the last Republican primary election in your precinct.
- obtain a list of precinct polling locations.
- obtain a list of favorable voters from your local traditional-values PAC.

### *Running for Precinct Chairperson*

#### How to organize

1. There are usually one hundred to five hundred people who vote for precinct chairperson. In most cases it only takes fifty to seventy-five votes to win. Eight-five percent of the people voting may not even know who is running for precinct chairperson.

2. Identify the people who will vote for you by going door-to-door and phoning. Start five weeks before the election.

3. About eight weeks before the primary, have printed 3¹/₂ by 8 inch cards with information on your family, where you

stand on the issues, and the date and polling place for the election. Print enough cards to give one to every potential voter in your precinct.

4. Ask five to ten friends to help you call the traditional-values voters in your precinct to let them know who you are. Keep a written record of the people called so your team can use it on election day for getting-out-the-vote.

5. You might want to set up some coffee parties in different neighborhoods. Ask a supporter to host a party and serve coffee, tea, and pastry at the meeting. Give those in attendance your campaign cards and get their names, addresses, and phone numbers. You might have a small box in sight for campaign donations.

6. The day before or on election day your phone team should call every voter you have identified as a potential supporter. Encourage each one to go to the polls.

7. You and your spouse and two volunteers might divide into two teams and be at the polls all day giving your information card to each voter. Remember, 7:00 A.M. until 10:00 A.M., noon hour, and 4:00 P.M. until 7:00 P.M. will be the heaviest voting times. If that is all you do, along with calling your friends, in most cases you will probably win. At polling locations you may talk to anyone in poll lines, but you must stay behind the markers that restrict campaign activities.

8. Whether you win or lose the election, be ready for your supporters to show up at the precinct convention and nominate you for precinct convention chairperson. Remember that everyone attending the precinct convention must have voted in the just-finished primary.

## Preparing for a Party Precinct Convention

Well in advance of the convention identify the traditional-values voters in your precinct who will support you for convention chairperson or who will support the resolutions you hope the convention will adopt. Generally speaking, those voters will not come to the precinct convention unless you ask them. Once you have them committed to support you, your job really starts.

1. Have a list of delegates you want to go to the senatorial convention prepared at least twenty-four hours before the precinct convention. You will have the opportunity to present that list during the convention. You should meet with the nomination committee, which meets one hour prior to the senatorial convention.

2. Discuss with your supporters who should be the permanent chairperson and secretary at the precinct convention convention and decide which supporters will make what motions.

3. Ask your supporters to be there thirty minutes before the convention begins. Meet them at the door, thank them for coming, and let them know who will be making motions.

4. When the meeting is called to order, count your supporters and determine if your group comprises the majority of voters in attendance.

5. If you have the majority, follow these steps: nominate and elect a permanent convention chairperson and secretary, nominate and elect your list of senatorial convention delegates, present and vote on resolutions, and adjourn. Obtain a list of all persons attending the precinct convention and all persons elected senatorial convention delegates and alternates.

6. If you do not have the majority, follow these steps: allow the election of the chairperson and secretary to proceed without opposition, move that all persons present be elected delegates (if the opposition nominates a slate of delegates before you do that, make a substitute motion that only and all those in attendance at the precinct convention be elected delegates to the senatorial convention) and move to adjourn. Obtain a list of all persons present and all persons elected delegates to the senatorial convention and have the permanent convention chairperson or secretary sign it.

Why move to nominate only and all those in attendance at the precinct convention as delegates to the senatorial convention?

Only those present at the precinct convention have expressed sufficient interest to merit consideration as delegates to the senatorial convention.

We should also be for party unity and progress. The fair thing is to give everyone present an equal voice.

### *Precinct Convention Order of Business*

Only those who have voted in the party primary are eligible to attend the precinct convention.

**Call to order.** The temporary convention chairperson will make the call to order. The precinct chairperson, acting as temporary chairperson of the convention, might say:

"It is now [time] P.M., the time set by the county Republican executive committee for the precinct convention to meet, accordingly, this convention of the Republican voters of Precinct [number] is now called to order."

The temporary chairperson might then say: "My name is _____. I am the party chairperson of Precinct [number], and I welcome all of you to this convention. I have asked [volunteer's name] to assist me by checking the credentials and supervising the signing in of those in attendance."

The voter registration card of each person must be checked for the stamp indicating that he or she voted either in person or absentee in the primary election. Latecomers may check in at any time; no quorum is necessary.

The temporary chairperson might then say: "I have also asked [volunteer's name] to serve as temporary secretary until a permanent secretary is elected and [volunteer's name] to serve as temporary sergeant-at-arms. The first business in order is the election of the permanent chairperson of this convention. I declare this meeting open for nominations for permanent chairperson."

If more than one person is nominated, the vote should be by division of the house (a standing vote). In a large convention, the temporary chairperson should appoint two people to count votes. Typically, the precinct chairperson is nominated and elected. If he or she is an ideological opponent, work to see that a chairperson who holds to biblical values is elected.

Nominations require a second. If there is only one nominee, the election can be by voice vote. If there is more than one nominee, the vote should be by division of the house. If there are more than two nominees, for the sake of saving time a rule can be adopted stating that after each division of the house, the nominee receiving the least votes be automatically withdrawn.

Note: The election is for chairperson of the convention only; not for party precinct chairperson. The party precinct chairperson is elected at the polls during a primary election.

After the election of the permanent convention chairperson and secretary the permanent chairperson might announce: "[Name] has been elected as permanent secretary. Will the list of persons in attendance at this convention be delivered now to the permanent secretary? The next business in order is the election of delegates and alternates to the party senatorial convention. Precinct [number] is entitled to [number] delegates and an equal number of alternates, all of whom must have voted in the Republican primary, in person or absentee."

From the floor someone might say: "Mr. Chairperson, I move to elect the following persons as delegates and alternates from precinct [number] to the senatorial convention." (He or she then reads from a list prepared in advance.)

The permanent chairperson might respond: "It has been moved and seconded that the following persons be elected as delegates and alternates from this precinct to the senatorial district/ county convention. Are you ready for the question? All in favor say "aye"; all opposed, say "no."

The convention secretary must record the address of each elected delegate and alternate in the convention minutes.

The nomination of delegates and alternates to the state convention is conducted in a similar manner. The precinct is allowed a specified number of delegates and an equal number of alternates.

The names of delegates nominated will be sent to the nominations committee of the senatorial district convention, and the actual delegates to the state convention will be elected at the senatorial convention.

The next precinct convention business is consideration of resolutions. Any person may introduce a resolution that is debatable and amendable. A majority vote is required for adoption.

Work to prepare and pass resolutions based on biblical beliefs and pro-family values. Prepare the resolutions in triplicate before the precinct convention, introduce your resolutions at the convention, and work for their passage. If they pass, they are sent to the senatorial convention; if they pass there, they are sent to the state convention for possible inclusion in the state party platform. You, and as many of your friends as possible, should try to get elected as delegates to the senatorial and state conventions so that you can work for the passage of your resolutions, choose pro-family party leadership, and vote for resolutions upholding traditional moral values.

It is the permanent convention chairperson's responsibility to see that an accurate written record is kept of convention proceedings, including the list of persons present and a list of delegates and alternates elected to the senatorial district convention and nominated to the state convention, with addresses and phone numbers included. A signed copy of that record should be available for copying by any convention participant for a period of thirty minutes immediately following adjournment. The chairperson must sign and transmit in person or by registered mail the convention record to the county clerk.

## A Sample Resolution

Below is a sample resolution that might be presented at a precinct convention. Other resolutions could pertain to family issues such as prayer in schools, home schooling, and the tax-exempt status of Christian schools.

WHEREAS the question of abortion continues to be a serious moral, and political issue;

AND WHEREAS many Americans are now forced to pay for government funded abortions against their consciences and against their free wills;

BE IT RESOLVED THAT THE _____ Party of _____ County, Precinct # — opposes the use of tax dollars for abortions and supports a constitutional amendment protecting innocent human life at every state of biological development; and

BE IT FURTHER RESOLVED that a copy of this resolution be forwarded to the district convention of the _____ party for consideration by that convention for submission to the state convention for the inclusion in the state and national platforms.

## The Senatorial District or County Convention

When you arrive at the district convention, go to the credentials table to get your badge. The convention hall will be divided according to precinct; signs will be clearly visible. Sit with your precinct.

*Important Convention Committees*

**Nominations committee** members are appointed by the temporary chairperson of the convention. The committee determines who should be at-large delegates to the state convention.

You will have the opportunity to present yourself to the nominations committee on two or three publicly announced occasions prior to the district convention to seek selection as an at-large delegate. If you have not done that before the convention, go to the room where the committee is meeting and make your presentation then.

Have a résumé of your party credentials ready with copies for each member of the committee. The résumé should mention your membership in Republican clubs, campaigns in which you have worked, and the volunteer positions you have held within those campaigns.

**The resolutions committee** may consider resolutions at the convention. Time will be a factor, so make your presentation brief. You may also speak in support of any resolution being considered by the committee.

During the general session of the convention the nominations committee chairperson will present a slate of delegates and alternates to the state convention for approval by the convention. The chairperson of the resolutions committee will also present the resolutions adopted by the committee for adoption by the convention. From the floor delegates may speak for or against those presentations and move to amend or table resolutions. So be ready to make your views known.

Resolutions will include those written on behalf of candidates seeking the office of committeeman and committeewoman, who are representatives from your senatorial district to the state Republican executive committee, the policy-making body of the state Republican party.

## The State Convention

### *Important Committees and Events at the State Convention*

**The credentials committee** at the state level, as at the senatorial district level, rules on the seating of delegates. It has the ability to disqualify any delegate or an entire delegation. Only the general session delegate vote can override the decisions of the credentials committee.

The credentials committee report will be the first order of business so it is a necessity to arrive at the state convention in time for the first session. Have favorable alternate delegates there ready to be seated if they are needed. At almost every state convention many alternates are seated, because of the number of absent delegates. So be sure to study your state's procedure for seating alternates.

**The congressional caucus** is used during presidential election years to nominate persons for national committeeman and woman. Those nominations will be taken to the convention floor.

The man and woman receiving the required number of nominations will be presented for a vote during the general session.

The national committeeman and woman from each state represent that state on the national Republican executive committee. This is the governing board for the national Republican party.

In nonpresidential election years you will be seated on the floor and caucus by senatorial district. Delegates will nominate and elect a man and woman to sit on the state Republican executive committee as a result of these caucuses. The state Republican executive committee (SREC) is a very important position in the party. To be effective, conservative Christians must have representatives on that committee.

**The rules committee** will consider changes in the rules of the Republican party of the state. Delegates may attend committee meetings.

**The resolutions committee** considers the resolutions brought forward from the senatorial district or county conventions for adoption into the state platform of the Republican party. Delegates may attend committee meetings, testify before the committee on behalf of resolutions, and offer additional resolutions.

During the convention's general session the chairperson and vice-chairperson of the state party is elected. Changes in rules are voted upon; resolutions adopted after debate; and other party business is considered.

State party conventions are also opportunities to attend activities such as receptions to meet political figures, prayer breakfasts, and rallies.

## An Overview of the Party System

### State Party

The state party oversees the budget, recruits candidates to run at the state convention, raises funds, hires employees, and maintains the file and data on past elections.

The board is made up of state executive committee members

elected at the state party convention in senatorial caucuses. Each senatorial caucus elects a man and woman to serve for two years to represent them on the board at no pay.

The state chairperson and vice chairperson are elected for nonpaying two-year terms by the general delegates at a state convention.

### National Committee

The national committee, located in Washington, oversees a large national budget, recruits candidates, maintains a staff, does research, and provides funds for party candidates.

The board of directors is elected every four years, concurrent with presidential elections, at the state convention. Nominations are made in congressional caucus and then presented to the general assembly for election. A man and a woman are elected to serve on the national board.

### Congressional Committee

Each party has a congressional committee. This committee is concerned with the U.S. congressional races only and governed by the sitting congressman. The congressional committee has a paid executive director and staff. The committee raises considerable money to help the candidate run for office, does research for sitting congressmen, and maintains data files on election, legislation, and other information important to congressmen.

### Senatorial Committee

The senatorial committee is concerned with the U.S. congressional races only and governed by sitting senators. The committee elects a chairperson from among themselves, has a paid executive director and staff, raises funds for the candidate, does research, maintains file on legislation and past elections, and works with the sitting senate.

# Technology at the Grassroots

**A** key to winning elections from the days of Lincoln to the present has been to collect useful information and build an effective organization. How can you accomplish that economically? One of the first things to do is to purchase an IBM compatible computer. The computer system might have the following features: a twenty-megabyte hard disc, two floppy disc drives, a modem, and a near-letter quality printer with letter and envelope feeder. Such a system should not cost over fifteen hundred dollars new.

Purchase software programs such as Pagemaker and Newsroom, which are two programs used for newsletters. There are also many campaign-related programs available, but most are rather costly. In any case, you will need a good database program that is user friendly so that any volunteers will be able to help with data input with minimal training and oversight. Our own organization developed an efficient computer program by modifying a software program in the public domain. Your computer system should be able to

- design different formats.
- sort your data in varied ways.
- retrieve specific data or data groups.

# Appendix C

- mail merge.
- perform word process functions for custom letter writing.
- import or export data from or to other systems by modem.
- create custom designed lists.

The more information you have available on voters, the better equipped you will be.

## Sample Letter

Refer to the user's manual of the software program you are using for instructions on how to merge data from different files. You may then wish to follow the format given below for creating letters for bulk mailings.

*[TITLE]  [FIRST]  [LAST]  [CODE]*
*[NUMBER]  [STR]*
*[CITY]  [ST]  [ZIP]*
  *Dear [SALUT];*
  *Thank you for your donation of [AMT] on [DATE]. We know you have been working hard for [ORG] this year. We need your help in this campaign. In the last election you volunteered to [VOL] for precinct [PRECINCT]. You also helped us set up a phone bank in your church, [CHURCH].*
  *We can provide you with a list of registered voters for your precinct.*
  *[SALUT], we hope we can count on you again.*
  *Sincerely,*

Everywhere in the letter I put brackets [ ] the computer is programed to insert the correct information, thus allowing me to write a personalized letter to everyone chosen from the computer file list. With a computer program that sorts, produces lists, word processes, runs spelling checks, and merges files, you too can produce that type of letter for your PAC.

Your computer can also "talk" to a mainframe computer in Washington, D.C., or a similar program at your state capital. Those systems of computer communications are available for a nominal fee. Such a capability tracks legislation, voting records, and financial reporting records. You might obtain specific information on legislation, determine whether your legislator is among the most liberal or the most conservative legislators, or see how they voted. Or, you might obtain information about what bills have been sent to committees, who their sponsors are, what committee they are in, who's on the committee, and who's chairperson of the committee.

You can create a state or county computer bulletin board for your PAC district director, area coordinator, or precinct coordinator so that they can inform their people of instruction and events by using a modem. Such modern communications technology will keep Christian grassroots America abreast of all political action in a timely fashion.

Remember, the information collected and stored is valuable to your organization and others. In Minnesota, a Christian political action group had its twenty-thousand-name member and Christian voter list stolen. They did not have backup discs, which was almost a deathblow to the group.

The following hints are important suggestions that may save your PAC time and avoid complications.

- Create a code to get into any sensitive file. Change the code every six months if necessary.
- Create two sets of backup discs of your computer files. Lock one set in a safe place apart from headquarters and keep one set on-site in case of computer or power failure.

## Automatic Dialing Machines

Another valuable communication tool is the automated dialing machine. Although automated telephone dialers are controversial, you will find that they are more dependable than volunteers. We have found that an automated dialing machine can do the work of twenty volunteers and provide accurate statistics of calls made. You may find that for under twenty dollars a month, an additional phone line for the dialing machine may be placed in a private home. Do some research before you invest in such machines. In most states you will be able to at least use the machines to call you PAC's own members.

COPAC has ten machines, each using a fifty-second message, which enables us to call approximately seven hundred houses per machine or seven thousand houses per day. Our machines are ETS 1500s, and they cost twelve hundred dollars each.

The ETS 1500 will

- upload or download directly from the computer databank. The software program costs approximately two hundred dollars.
- have a voice computer chip, which has no delay when someone answers.
- use a prerecorded tape of a candidate or personality on a message chip.
- keep a record by telephone number of all calls made. It will make a record of calls completed, calls not answered, or hang ups; it will recall numbers that were busy or had no response; and it will record what the person answering has to say.

We have found out, as many have, that the automatic dialer is a perfect tool, because it can call anywhere, doesn't need a break, doesn't get down when people respond negatively, and doesn't waste time with conversation.

We have used automated dialing systems to

- do polling.
- contact volunteers and advise leaders.
- do hotline updates for pastors.
- notify the Christian community of legislative issues or educate them about a candidate.
- raise funds.
- deliver get-out-the-vote messages on election day.

Automated callers have their time and place, and once your members know what to expect, they begin to look forward to receiving the information. Many have frowned when automated calling machines are mentioned, but such technology is an efficient, inexpensive modern-day means of communication.

## Using Technology to Recruit Precinct Chairpersons

In 1988, COPAC used computer data and the automated dialing machines before the Republican primary to recruit people to run for party precinct chairperson. There were 341 precinct chairperson positions in our county. There were 183 precincts that currently had precinct chairpersons. That left 158 positions vacant. From our research of Republican records of the past ten years we found that 92 percent of the 158 precinct chairperson positions had never been filled, were primarily in black, hispanic, and lower-income areas. Because our computer files contained names from charismatic, independent, and evangelical churches, as well as pro-life groups, we knew the majority of the voters listed in our data bank voted Republican.

Using a report that the election commission had given us, our volunteers were able to look up the precinct numbers of the majority of Christian voters in our data bank. We then sorted the names alphabetically by precinct and made a printout, which listed each precinct and the names of Judeo-Christian, traditional-values voters in each precinct. The list also showed us those who had done volunteer work and given financially.

We sent computer-generated letters to each name on our list. The letter contained information about the duties of party precinct chairperson, how to run for the office, and what data our PAC could furnish. We also let them know that we would help in their training. We also used an automated dialer to call people in each precinct and invite them to a meeting for a briefing on the responsibilities of a party precinct chairperson. From those efforts we had 138 people fill out forms to file for party precinct chairpersons. In party elections eighty-seven of our people did not have an opponent.

☆ **207** ☆

We then provided our precinct chairperson candidates with name lists for their precincts and computer-generated personalized letters for each individual. We used the automated dialers to communicate and had training sessions on precinct convention procedures. We averaged over two hundred people at each session. We also created a "how to" videotape on participating in a precinct convention and furnished copies to our candidates.

The results were overwhelming. Thirty out of the fifty-one opposed candidates won, and we passed a pro-family resolution at every precinct but two. In addition, we also saw a 300 percent increase in the number of minority persons participating in the precinct conventions. Such results serve as one example of how technology can affect grassroots politics.

## Satellite Links and Video Programs

There were several new technological innovations used by the Christian political community in 1988. Richie Martin, the director of Pat Robertson's primary presidential campaign in Texas, wanted to build up his network of volunteers. To do that the Robertson campaign and its supporters organized three hundred locations to receive satellite-relayed television broadcasts. The Robertson campaign then broadcast a one-hour campaign program, originating from Dallas, to those three hundred statewide locations. In addition, several campaign headquarters on the East Coast used the same broadcast to reach their supporters.

The Robertson campaign used the satellite-transmitted program as a fund-raising and volunteer recruitment tool. They raised over sixty thousand dollars and recruited over forty thousand volunteer names in Texas alone, using a campaign tactic that requested each person viewing the broadcast to ask eight reliable people to recruit eight more volunteers.

Ronald Reagan had used a similar method in 1986 by simply going across the street from the White House to the National Chamber of Commerce television studios and broadcasting live to several states and endorsing various candidates. He was able to raise thousands of dollars and help several candidates all in one hour, without ever leaving Washington.

Richie Martin repeated the same satellite-link technology during the 1988 Texas Supreme Court races. The Texas Supreme Court elections normally receive very little attention, even though Texas Supreme Court seats are some of the most powerful elected positions in the state.

Martin is now developing Starnet. Starnet will produce programs that focus on national and state politicians and legislative issues, and for a small fee your PAC can receive the broadcasts for use during PAC precinct meetings. Think of it, with today's technology a PAC precinct coordinator can have a hundred-thousand-dollar campaign program available exclusively for the voters in his or her precinct. Using the latest technology, Starnet will enable a person at the precinct level to communicate with nationally known speakers. PAC members will be inspired and want to assist their leaders in grassroots fund-raising and the recruiting of volunteers.

Video programs, satellite links, computers, and automated dialing machines are not out of your PAC's budget. On the contrary, the use of such technology will inspire people to give a larger amount of their money locally. They will sooner understand how their involvement in the political system can determine their local and state elections.

# A Biblical Study: Leadership, Morality, and Freedom

There are two world views at war in American public policy today. One is the Judeo-Christian world view based on the Bible and the other is the secular humanist world view based on human wisdom.[1]

Those world views offer a foundation on which a godly or an ungodly lifestyle can be developed. The humanist lifestyle is based on situation ethics, but the Judeo-Christian lifestyle of Bible believers is based on an understanding of the Scriptures.

Applying teaching from the Bible to one's personal life doesn't offend most humanists, but when Christians want to apply biblical principles and teachings to public policy, secular humanists scream about a violation of the separation of church and

---

1. The material in this section is taken from *Biblical Scoreboard*, Fall 1988, pp. 8–9. David Balsinger, the president of *Biblical Scoreboard*, has authored many books and is one of the most brilliant and innovative minds of the Christian movement.

state, claim the Bible is not relevant to contemporary issues, and accuse Christians of presuming to speak for God. Secular humanists fail to realize that America is great because devout Christians and courageous politicians have used biblical values to shape our political institutions. America is not the product of secular humanism, atheism, or any other false religion. America *is* the fruit of God's eternal truth in Christ, the Ten Commandments, and responsible politicians.

## Some of the Issues

Listed below are Scriptures dealing with a number of current public policy issues. These passages will help you discover what God thinks and provide the biblical principles on which public policy should be based. You might use these Scriptures to guide personal spiritual growth or as scriptural support for a church Bible study group.

## Abortion

*For thou didst form my inward parts; thou didst weave me in my mother's womb. I will give thanks to thee for I am fearfully and wonderfully made: wonderful are thy works, and my soul knows it very well. My frame was not hidden from thee, when I was made in secret, and skillfully wrought in the depths of the earth. Thine eyes have seen my unformed substance; and in thy book they were all written, the days that were ordained for me, when as yet there was not one of them* (Ps. 139:13–16 NASB).

| | |
|---|---|
| Genesis 1:27 | Deuteronomy 5:17 |
| Genesis 9:6 | Deuteronomy 27:17, 19, 25 |
| Exodus 2:2–3 | Deuteronomy 30:19 |
| Exodus 20:13 | 2 Kings 21:6 |
| Exodus 21:22–23 | Job 31:15 |
| Exodus 23:7 | Psalm 100:3 |
| Numbers 35:33 | Psalm 106:38 |

| | |
|---|---|
| Psalm 113:9 | Jeremiah 7:31 |
| Psalm 127:3–5 | Hosea 9:11 |
| Psalm 128:3–4 | Matthew 2:18 |
| Proverbs 6:16–19 | Matthew 18:1–6 |
| Proverbs 24:11–12 | Matthew 18:10 |
| Ecclesiastes 11:5 | Matthew 19:14 |
| Isaiah 5:20–21 | Matthew 25:44–45 |
| Isaiah 8:18 | Luke 1:41–44 |
| Isaiah 44:24 | Luke 18:15–17 |
| Isaiah 49:1 | Romans 12:2 |
| Isaiah 59:7 | Galatians 1:15–16 |
| Jeremiah 1:5 | |

# AIDS

*For this reason God gave them over to degrading passions; for their women exchanged the natural function for that which is unnatural, and in the same way also the men abandoned the natural function of the woman and burned in their desire towards one another, men with men committing indecent acts and receiving in their own persons the due penalty of their error* (Rom. 1:26–27 NASB).

| | |
|---|---|
| Exodus 15:26 | 2 Chronicles 21:18 |
| Leviticus 26:21 | Ezekiel 18:26–28 |
| Deuteronomy 7:15 | Galatians 6:7–8 |
| Deuteronomy 28:58–62 | James 1:14–15 |

## Fiscal Responsibility

*The rich rules over the poor, and the borrower is the slave of the lender* (Prov. 22:7 NASB).

*For which of you, intending to build a tower, does not sit down first and count the cost, whether he has enough to finish it—lest, after he has laid the foundation, and is not able to finish it, all who see it begin to mock him* (Luke 14:28–30 NKJV).

| | |
|---|---|
| Leviticus 19:36 | Proverbs 11:1 |
| Deuteronomy 25:13–15 | Proverbs 16:11 |
| Psalm 37:21 | Proverbs 17:18 |
| Proverbs 6:1–3 | Proverbs 22:3–4 |

☆ **213** ☆

Proverbs 22:26–27          Romans 13:6–7
Proverbs 27:23–24          1 Peter 2:13–14
Romans 13:1–2

## Capital Punishment

*And if a man takes the life of any human being, he shall surely be put to death* (Lev. 24:17 NASB).

Genesis 9:4–6, 12          Deuteronomy 24:7
Exodus 21:12–15            Ecclesiastes 8:11
Exodus 21:16               Luke 23:40–41
Exodus 21:23–25            Acts 25:10–12
Leviticus 24:17–21         Romans 13:3–4
Numbers 16:9–34            James 1:14–15
Deuteronomy 21:22

## Creationism

*Thou alone art the Lord. Thou hast made the heavens, the heaven of heavens with all their host, the earth and all that is on it, the seas and all that is in them. Thou dost give life to all of them . . .* (Neh. 9:6 NASB).

Genesis 1:1                Malachi 2:10
Genesis 1:24–27          . John 1:1–3
Exodus 20:11               Acts 17:24–26
Psalm 33:6–9               Romans 1:25
Psalm 115:15               Hebrews 11:3, 6
Isaiah 44:2

## Drug and Alcohol Abuse

*There shall not be found among you any one who burns his son or his daughter as an offering, anyone who practices divination, a soothsayer, or an augur, or a sorcerer,[2] or a charmer, or a medium, or a wizard, or a necromancer* (Deut. 18:10–11 RSV).

---

2. Sorcery *(pharmakela)* in Greek means "enchantment with drugs," and sorcerers *(pharmakeus)* "enchanters with drugs."

| | |
|---|---|
| Proverbs 20:1 | 1 Corinthians 6:9–11 |
| Proverbs 23:20–21 | 1 Corinthians 6:19–20 |
| Proverbs 31:4–5 | Galatians 5:16–21 |
| Habakkuk 2:15 | Ephesians 5:18 |
| Malachi 3:5 | James 1:14–15 |
| Romans 13:13 | 2 Peter 2:19 |
| 1 Corinthians 3:16–17 | Revelation 18:23 |
| 1 Corinthians 5:11 | Revelation 21:7–8 |

## Education

*All Scripture is inspired by God and profitable for teaching, for reproof, for correction, for training in righteousness* (2 Tim. 3:16 NASB).

| | |
|---|---|
| Deuteronomy 4:10 | Isaiah 28:9 |
| Deuteronomy 6:7 | Hosea 4:6 |
| Deuteronomy 11:18–23 | Habakkuk 2:14 |
| Proverbs 1:8–9 | Matthew 10:24 |
| Proverbs 4:1–2 | Romans 10:17 |
| Proverbs 6:20–23 | Romans 15:4 |
| Proverbs 22:6 | 2 Timothy 3:15 |

## Pro-Family Values

*And the Lord God said, "It isn't good for man to be alone; I will make a companion for him, a helper suited to his needs"* (Gen. 2:18 TLB).

| | |
|---|---|
| Genesis 1:27–28 | Colossians 3:18–21 |
| Genesis 2:21–24 | 1 Timothy 5:8 |
| Psalm 107:41 | Titus 2:3–5 |
| Psalm 127:3–5 | Hebrews 13:4 |
| Proverbs 18:22 | 1 Peter 3:6–7 |
| Ephesians 5:22–30 | |

## Euthanasia

*There are six things which the Lord hates, yes seven which are an abomination to Him: haughty eyes, a lying tongue, hands*

☆ **215** ☆

*that shed innocent blood, a heart that devises wicked plans, feet that run rapidly to evil, a false witness who utters lies, and one who spreads strife among brothers* (Prov. 6:16–19 NASB).

| | |
|---|---|
| Genesis 9:6 | Proverbs 16:31 |
| Exodus 20:12 | Proverbs 23:22 |
| Exodus 20:13 | Isaiah 3:5 |
| Exodus 23:7 | Matthew 5:21 |
| Leviticus 19:32 | Matthew 18:10 |
| Leviticus 24:17 | Matthew 19:14 |
| Deuteronomy 30:15–19 | John 10:10 |
| Psalm 8:2 | 1 Corinthians 3:16–17 |
| Psalm 139:13–17 | |

## Faith and Morality

### Faith

*You shall fear only the Lord your God and you shall worship Him, and swear by His name* (Deut. 6:13 NASB).

### Morality

*When the righteous increase, the people rejoice, but when a wicked man rules, people groan* (Prov. 29:2 NASB).

| | |
|---|---|
| Exodus 18:21 | Zechariah 1:3–4 |
| Deuteronomy 16:18–19 | Zechariah 7:9–10 |
| 2 Chronicles 7:14 | Zechariah 8:16 |
| Psalm 33:12 | John 5:39–40 |
| Proverbs 20:6 | Romans 1:17 |
| Proverbs 20:28 | Romans 10:17 |
| Proverbs 21:15 | 2 Corinthians 13:5 |
| Proverbs 29:4 | Ephesians 6:16 |
| Ezekiel 33:2–6 | Philippians 2:15 |
| Hosea 10:2 | Hebrews 12:2 |
| Hosea 10:12 | James 2:17–20 |
| Micah 6:8 | 1 Timothy 2:1–2 |

## Homosexuality

*Don't you know that the wicked will not inherit the kingdom of God. Do not be deceived: Neither the sexually immoral nor idolaters nor adulterers nor male prostitutes nor homosexual of-fenders nor thieves nor the greedy nor drunkards nor slanderers nor swindlers will inherit the kingdom of God* (1 Cor. 6:9–10 NIV).

| | |
|---|---|
| Genesis 1:27 | Romans 1:24–32 |
| Genesis 19:4–5, 24 | 1 Timothy 1:9–11 |
| Leviticus 18:22 | 2 Peter 2:6 |
| Leviticus 20:13 | Jude 1:7 |
| 1 Kings 14:24 | |

## Infanticide

*"See that you do not despise one of these little ones, for I say to you, that their angels in heaven continually behold the face of my Father who is in heaven."*

*"Thus it is not the will of your Father who is in heaven that one of these little ones perish"* (Matt. 18:10, 14 NASB).

| | |
|---|---|
| 2 Kings 17:16–20 | Jeremiah 22:3 |
| Psalm 127:3 | Matthew 25:37–40 |
| Proverbs 24:11–12 | |

## Loans and Usury

*Do not be among those who give pledges, among those who become sureties for debt* (Prov. 22:26 NASB).

*Avoid getting into debt, except the debt of mutual love* (Rom. 13:8 JERUSALEM BIBLE).

| | |
|---|---|
| 2 Kings 4:7 | Ezekiel 18:5–9 |
| Psalm 15:5 | Luke 6:34 |
| Proverbs 11:15 | 1 Corinthians 5:11 |
| Proverbs 17:18 | |

## National Security

*These people all trusted God and as a result won battles, overthrew kingdoms, ruled their people well, and received what*

*God had promised them; they were kept from harm in a den of lions, and in a fiery furnace* (Heb. 11:33–34 TLB).

| | |
|---|---|
| Leviticus 26:1–8 | Ezekiel 22:30 |
| 2 Samuel 22:47–48 | Ezekiel 33:2–6 |
| 2 Chronicles 11:5, 11 | Zechariah 4:6 |
| 2 Chronicles 26:9–15 | Matthew 12:29 |
| Psalm 120:6–7 | Matthew 24:7–14, 43–44 |
| Isaiah 25:3 | Luke 14:31 |
| Isaiah 28:15–18 | Luke 22:35–38 |
| Jeremiah 1:18–19 | Romans 12:18 |
| Jeremiah 51:20 | 2 Corinthians 6:14 |

## Parental Consent and Birth Control

*Children, obey your parents in the Lord, for this is right. Honor your father and mother . . . And, fathers, do not provoke your children to anger; but bring them up in the discipline and instruction of the Lord* (Eph. 6:1–2, 4 NASB).

| | |
|---|---|
| Genesis 16:9 | Proverbs 22:6 |
| Exodus 20:12 | Proverbs 22:15 |
| Numbers 36:6 | Proverbs 23:13–14 |
| Deuteronomy 11:18–19 | Proverbs 29:15 |
| 1 Samuel 18:20–21 | 1 Corinthians 7:36–38 |
| Proverbs 4:1–5 | Colossians 3:20–21 |
| Proverbs 6:20–23 | Hebrews 12:11 |
| Proverbs 19:18 | |

## Pornography

*But do not let immorality or any impurity or greed even be named among you, as is proper among saints; and there must be no filthiness and silly talk, or coarse jesting, which are not fitting, but rather giving of thanks. For this you know with certainty, that no immoral or impure person or covetous man, who is an idolater, has an inheritance in the kingdom of Christ and God* (Eph. 5:3–5 NASB).

# Bible Study

Job 31:1
Ezekiel 23:14, 20
Matthew 5:27-28
Mark 7:20-23
Romans 1:21-32
Romans 13:13-14
1 Corinthians 3:16-17
1 Corinthians 6:9-10
2 Corinthians 12:21
Galatians 5:19-21

Ephesians 4:19-24
Ephesians 5:11-12
1 Thessalonians 5:22
1 Timothy 1:9-10
2 Timothy 2:22
1 Peter 2:11
1 Peter 4:3-5
2 Peter 2:14
1 John 2:16-17

## Religious Freedom

*Now the Lord is the Spirit; and where the Spirit of the Lord is, there is liberty* (2 Cor. 3:17 NASB).

Exodus 19:5-6
Deuteronomy 5:7-11
Deuteronomy 6:4-25
Esther 3:8-9
Esther 8:11
Psalm 2:1-2
Psalm 102:18-22
Isaiah 42:6-7

Daniel 3:13-18, 28-29
Matthew 23:13
Luke 4:18-19
Acts 4:17-20
Acts 17:26-28
Romans 6:14-16
Ephesians 6:11-12
1 Timothy 2:1-2

## Secular Humanism

*So it was that when they gave God up and would not even acknowledge him, God gave them up to doing everything their evil minds could think of. Their lives became full of every kind of wickedness and sin . . . They were backbiters, haters of God, insolent, proud braggarts, always thinking of new ways of sinning . . . (Rom. 1:28-30 TLB).*

Isaiah 40:28
Isaiah 55:8-9
Jeremiah 17:9
Daniel 2:20
Hosea 4:6-7

Romans 12:2
1 Corinthians 1:18-21
1 Corinthians 1:25
1 Corinthians 3:19
2 Corinthians 4:3-6

☆ **219** ☆

Ephesians 4:14–18　　　　　James 1:5
Philippians 2:5–7　　　　　　1 John 2:15–16
2 Timothy 3:1–9

## Taxation

*Then there was a great outcry from the people and their wives. Our sons and daughters are a great number, let us get grain, so we may have food for our needs. We are giving our fields and vine gardens for debt . . . We have given our fields and vine gardens to get money for the King's taxes, yet we are forcing our sons and daughters to be slaves . . . we can do nothing about it* (Neh. 5:1–5 NASB).

2 Kings 23:35　　　　　　　Mark 12:14–17
2 Chronicles 10:6–10　　　　Luke 2:1–5
Ezra 4:20　　　　　　　　　Romans 13:6–7
Isaiah 47:6

## Trade

*Should you help the wicked and love those who hate the LORD? Therefore the wrath of the LORD is upon you* (2 Chron. 19:2 NKJV).

2 Kings 20:12–17　　　　　　Proverbs 31:24
2 Chronicles 16:3–9　　　　　Isaiah 5:20–24
Psalm 107:23–24　　　　　　Isaiah 28:15
Psalm 118:8–9　　　　　　　Matthew 25:16–18

## Voluntary Prayer

*Now He was telling them a parable to show that at all times they ought to pray and not to lose heart* (Luke 18:1 NASB).

1 Samuel 12:23　　　　　　　Proverbs 15:33
Psalm 5:1–3　　　　　　　　Proverbs 16:6
Proverbs 15:8　　　　　　　Proverbs 22:6
Proverbs 15:29　　　　　　　Daniel 6:10

# Bible Study

Matthew 19:13–14

Matthew 21:22

Romans 12:12

Ephesians 6:18–19

1 Thessalonians 5:17

1 Timothy 2:1

2 Timothy 2:8